Excel
Basic Skills

Times Tables 1

2-3 Years
Ages 7-9

Get the Results You Want!

Bev Dunbar

PASCAL
PRESS

© 2000 Bev Dunbar and Pascal Press
Reprinted 2001, 2002, 2003, 2004, 2005, 2006, 2007, 2008, 2010

Updated in 2012 for the Australian Curriculum

Reprinted 2013, 2014, 2015, 2017, 2018, 2019, 2020, 2022

ISBN 978 1 74020 029 5

Pascal Press
PO Box 250
Glebe NSW 2037
(02) 8585 4044
www.pascalpress.com.au

Publisher: Vivienne Joannou
Project editors: Mark Dixon and May McCool
Edited by Heather Cam and May McCool
Answers checked by Peter Little
Page design and typesetting by Janart Design Studio and Precision Typesetting (Barbara Nilsson)
Cover by DiZign Pty Ltd
Printed by Vivar Printing/Green Giant Press

Riddles adapted from:
A Bag Full of Riddles, Lamont Publishing, Australia, 1993.

The images used herein were obtained from:
IMSI's MasterClips Collection
1875 Francisco Blvd
San Rafael
CA 94901-5506
USA.

Contents

INTRODUCTION *for Parents*

Multiplication is one of the basic skills in Mathematics that all children need to know. As a parent, you want your child to learn their 'tables' in an enjoyable way and you also want your child to develop quick recall of all the facts.

This book reviews the basic multiplication facts for × 2, × 10, × 5, doubling, × 1, × 0, × 3 and × 4. A second book, *Excel Basic Skills Times Tables 2 Years 3–4*, covers the basic multiplication facts for × 6, × 7, × 8, × 9, × 11 and × 12.

This book will help your child succeed at their 'tables' for the following reasons:

- There is an emphasis on oral counting.
- There is an emphasis on language.
- Each unit is carefully sequenced to assist mathematical learning.
- The discovery of patterns is encouraged.
- A wide variety of activities are provided.
- Your child will regularly apply the facts to real-life problems.

By practising multiplication at home, your child will reinforce learning in the classroom. Don't expect them to remember everything after only a few experiences, however. Practice will make perfect!

When discussing multiplication with your child, it's best to start with terms like 'groups of' or 'rows of', using real objects, pictures and drawings.

After the × sign is introduced, you can then practise in a more formal way, recording multiplication using the symbols.

After much practice, your child will reach the 'Quick Recall' stage, where they are able to remember their multiplication facts on demand. Regular 'Beat the Clock' challenges allow your child to graph their progress in this area. You will also find Quick Questions scattered throughout the book, at the bottom of a page. These challenge your child to think flexibly and use their growing multiplication or division knowledge to solve problems.

Once the facts in this book have been mastered, your child will be ready to tackle the challenges of the next book in the *Excel* Basic Skills series. They will then be well equipped to solve more complex multiplication problems in Years 4–6 and beyond.

To help you reward your child's progress, use 'My Progress Chart' at the back of this book. Colour one star for every page completed, or two stars if everything on the page is correct. Colour three stars for each correct 'Check-up' page.

Set 1: Groups of 2

1 What can you count that comes in twos?
(For example, wings, eyes, hands, legs) ....

How many wings on this bee?

2   1 group of 2 wings

2 How many wings on 3 bees?

2 + ... + ...3..... groups of 2 wings

---

How many wheels on this bike?

2   1 group of 2 wheels

3 How many wheels on 4 bikes?

2 + ... + ... + ... groups of 2 wheels

How many eyes on this fish?

2   1 group of 2 eyes

4 How many eyes on 5 fish?

2 + ... + ... + ... + ... groups of 2 eyes

---

How many legs altogether on 2 children, 2 babies and 2 grandmas?

....

Set 2: Rows of 2

You can sort things into equal rows of 2.
This makes a 2s array.
This is what 10 rows of 2 hippos look like as an array.

---

1 Draw 3 rows of
2 circles as an array.

2 Draw 5 rows of
2 triangles as an array.

3 Draw 7 rows of
2 rectangles as an array.

4 Draw 9 rows of 2 sticks
as an array.

---

5 This is what 10 equal groups of 2 look like on a number line.

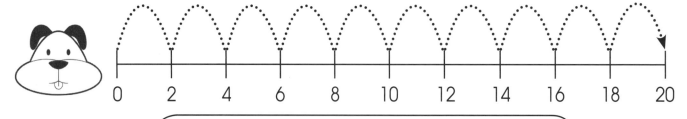

Draw in your own jumps of 2 on this number line, starting at 0 and finishing at 20.

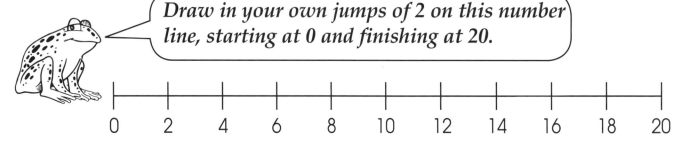

Set 3: Find the Groups of 2

How many objects in each picture?
How many groups of 2 can you find? Draw a circle around each group of 2.

1

.... groups of 2 shapes

2

.... groups of 2 shapes

3

.... groups of 2 shapes

4

.... groups of 2 shapes

5

.... groups of 2 shapes

6

.... groups of 2 shapes

Set 4: What a Lot of Ears!

How many ears on 1 dog?
There is one group of two ears.

That makes | **2** | ears altogether.

---

1 How many ears on 4 dogs?
There are 4 groups of 2 ears.

That makes | | ears altogether.

---

2 How many ears on 6 dogs?
There are 6 groups of 2 ears.

That makes | | ears altogether.

---

3 How many ears on 9 dogs?
There are 9 groups of 2 ears.

That makes | |
ears altogether.

---

4 How many ears altogether on all the dogs on this page?

There are | | groups of 2 ears.   That makes | | ears altogether.

Set 5: Counting by Twos

1 Count by 2 to fill in the missing numbers on these ladders.
Start at the bottom of each ladder.

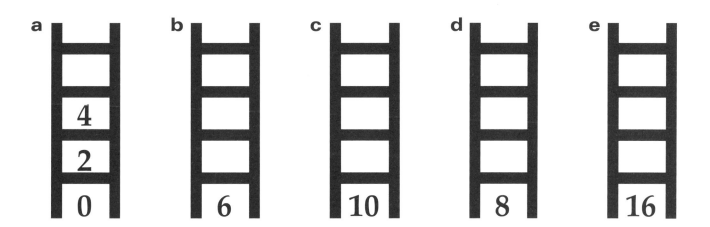

2 Can you count backwards by 2s from 20?

20   18   ....

3 Join up all the dots to show how you count by 2.

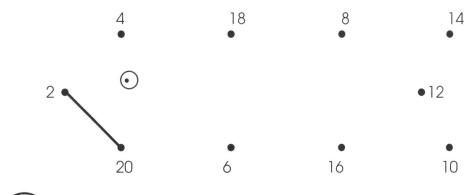

Can you count backwards by 2?
Start at 30 and count to 20.
Start at 40 and count to 30.
Start at 50 and count to 40.

Set 6: What a Lot of Socks!

How many socks in a pair?   2 | 1 | group of 2

1 in 2 pairs?   .... | 2 | groups of 2

2 in 3 pairs?   .... | | groups of 2

3 in 4 pairs?   .... | | groups of 2

4 in 5 pairs?   .... | | groups of 2

5 in 6 pairs?   .... | | groups of 2

6 in 7 pairs?   .... | | groups of 2

7 in 8 pairs?   .... | | groups of 2

8 in 9 pairs?   .... | | groups of 2

9 in 10 pairs?   .... | | groups of 2

10 What is the pattern? ....

....

11 How many pairs of shoes do you own? | | groups of 2

How many shoes altogether? ....

> *How many pairs of shoes does your whole family own?*
> *How many shoes altogether?*
>
> ....

Set 7: What a Lot of Legs!

How many legs?

Guess first: ....

To find the total number of legs we can:

count them one by one	1 2 3 4 5 6 7 8 9 10 11 12
count them by twos	2 4 6 8 10 12
add up all the twos	2 + 2 + 2 + 2 + 2 + 2

Which do you think is the easiest way?

There are 6 groups of 2 legs.
There are 12 legs altogether.

We can write this as: 6 groups of 2 = 12
Or we can write: 2 + 2 + 2 + 2 + 2 + 2 = 12

Multiplication is another easy way to add the same number each time.
It's shorter to write.
This is the special sign to show we are multiplying → X
Use this sign instead of writing 'groups of'.

We can now write: 6 × 2 = 12

How do we write:
4 groups of 2 equal 8? ....

7 groups of 2 equal 14? ....

Set 8: Counting Balls

How many balls?

    3 groups of 2 balls $3 \times 2 = 6$

1 Draw your own picture to show:

6 groups of 2 balls $6 \times 2 = $ ☐

2 Fill in the missing parts to show:

 ☐ groups of 2 balls   ☐ $\times 2 = $ ☐

3 Look for a pattern.
Colour in all the numbers as you count by 2.

1	2	3	4	5	6	7	8	9	10
11	12	13	14	15	16	17	18	19	20
21	22	23	24	25	26	27	28	29	30
31	32	33	34	35	36	37	38	39	40
41	42	43	44	45	46	47	48	49	50
51	52	53	54	55	56	57	58	59	60
61	62	63	64	65	66	67	68	69	70
71	72	73	74	75	76	77	78	79	80
81	82	83	84	85	86	87	88	89	90
91	92	93	94	95	96	97	98	99	100

4 What pattern can you see in the final digits?

....

5 What is the fourth number in the 2s pattern?

....

6 What is the tenth number in this pattern?

....

How many groups of 2 balls in 18 balls?

....

Set 9: Mix and Match

How many sticks?

‖ ‖   2 × 2 = 4

Write the matching multiplication name for these pictures.

1 ‖ ‖ ‖ ‖ ‖ ‖ ‖ ‖ ‖   ☐ × 2 = ...

2 ‖ ‖ ‖ ‖   ☐ × 2 = ...

3 Draw your own pictures of sticks to match the four questions below.
Write the answer.

a 7 × 2 = ...	**b** 5 × 2 = ...
c 10 × 2 = ...	**d** 1 × 2 = ...

4 Finish this pattern.

2   4   6   ....

5 You may like to use this pattern or draw a picture to help answer these:

a 4 × 2 = ...   **b** 3 × 2 = ...   **c** 5 × 2 = ...   **d** 10 × 2 = ...

e 1 × 2 = ...   **f** 7 × 2 = ...   **g** 9 × 2 = ...   **h** 6 × 2 = ...

Circle the easiest one to remember.
Put a line under the hardest one to remember.

Four children have $2 each. How much money is there altogether?

....

Set 10: Match Them Up

1 Draw a line to show the matching dogs and bones.
Be careful—there will be two bones left over!

2 Circle the number which is the answer to the number sentence.

a 5 × 2 = 12 10 8 7	**b** 4 × 2 = 12 7 10 8
c 7 × 2 = 6 9 14 12	**d** 8 × 2 = 16 18 14 10

3 Count backwards by 2s. Fill in the missing numbers.

4 Write the matching number names.

2 + 2 + 2 + 2	4 groups of 2	4 × 2	8
a	7 groups of 2	....	....
b	.... groups of	1 × 2	....
c	.... groups of	....	6
d	.... groups of	5 × 2	

There are 14 people dancing.
How many pairs are there? ....

Set 11: Challenge

1 Time yourself to see how quickly you can find the answers.

a $5 \times 2 =$ .... **b** $8 \times 2 =$ .... **c** $3 \times 2 =$ .... **d** $10 \times 2 =$ ....

e $1 \times 2 =$ .... **f** $4 \times 2 =$ .... **g** $7 \times 2 =$ .... **h** $2 \times 2 =$ ....

Number of seconds ....

Can you answer these without using any fingers or pictures to help you?

2 Beat the clock

a Can you fill in this grid in less than 90 seconds?

×	6	10	5	8	1	3	9	2	7	4
2										

Number of seconds ....

b Can you fill in this grid in less than 80 seconds?

×	3	8	1	7	10	2	6	5	4	9
2										

Number of seconds ....

c Can you fill in this grid in less than 70 seconds?

×	10	1	4	8	3	6	7	9	2	5
2										

Number of seconds ....

Cat food is $2 a tin.
I paid $18.
How many tins did I buy? ....

Set 12: Mind Munchers

Write the number sentence to match each story.

1 10 pineapples at $2 each.
How much altogether?

.... × .... = ...

2 5 dogs with 2 spots each.
How many spots?

.... × .... = ...

3 4 bikes with 2 wheels each.
How many wheels?

.... × .... = ...

4 I have 2 legs, you have 2 legs
and my friend has 2 legs.
How many legs altogether?

.... × .... = ...

Challenge

5 Each person has 2 eyes.
There are 14 eyes altogether.
How many people are there?

.... × .... = ...

6 There are 16 socks.
How many pairs are there?

.... × .... = ...

7 Make up your own number story and write it here: ....

....

Now write the number sentence for your story. .... × .... = ...

Each big dog has two puppies.
There are 20 puppies.
How many big dogs are there? ....

Excel Basic Skills *Times Tables 1 Years 2–3* Unit 1

Set 13: Check-up

How much do you remember about multiplying by 2s?

1 How many groups?

a .... groups of ....

b .... groups of ....

2 Draw a picture to match.

a 6 × 2

b 9 × 2

3 Draw a line to the correct answer.

7 × 2	6	3 × 2		10 × 2	
			18		
					6 × 2
				10	
9 × 2	20		12		
					14

4 Continue these counting patterns.

a 8 10 12 ....

b 20 18 16 ....

5 Do these quickly. Can you do them in less than 90 seconds?

a 3 × 2 = ...   **b** 6 × 2 = ...   **c** 7 × 2 = ...   **d** 10 × 2 = ...

e 5 × 2 = ...   **f** 8 × 2 = ...   **g** 4 × 2 = ...   **h** 1 × 2 = ...

Number of seconds ....

The children all took their shoes off. There are now 16 shoes in a pile. How many children are there? ....

Set 1: Groups of 10

Counting by 10s is easy.
Perhaps it is because we all have 10 fingers.

1 What else can you count that comes in tens?

....

2 How many fingers do you have?

10

1 group of .... fingers

| 10 |

3 How many fingers do 2 people have?

10 + 10

.... groups of .... fingers

4 How many toes do 3 people have?

10 + 10 + 10

.... groups of .... toes

5 What pattern can you see? ....

....

6 Write how you count by 10.

10   20   30   ....

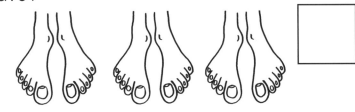

How many fingers and toes do 3 people have altogether?

....

Set 2: Rows of 10

You can sort things into equal rows of 10 to make a 10s array. The things line up in rows and columns. This is what 10 rows of 10 bugs look like as an array.

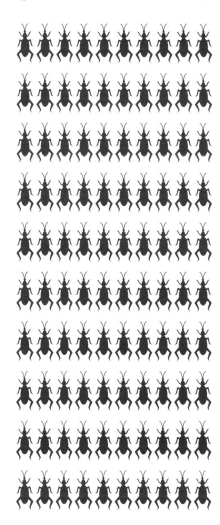

1 Draw 2 rows of 10 squares as an array.

2 Draw 4 rows of 10 pentagons as an array.

3 Draw 6 rows of 10 hexagons as an array.

4 Draw 8 rows of 10 dots as an array.

5 This is what 10 equal groups of 10 look like on a number line.

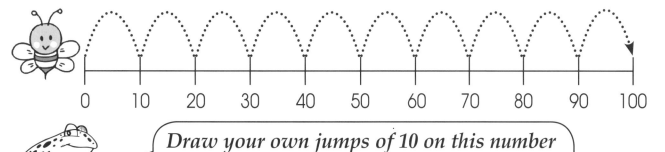

Draw your own jumps of 10 on this number line, starting at 0 and finishing at 100.

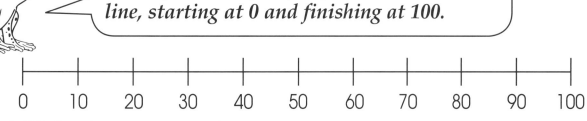

Set 3: Rows of 10

Colour in the rows to show the following:

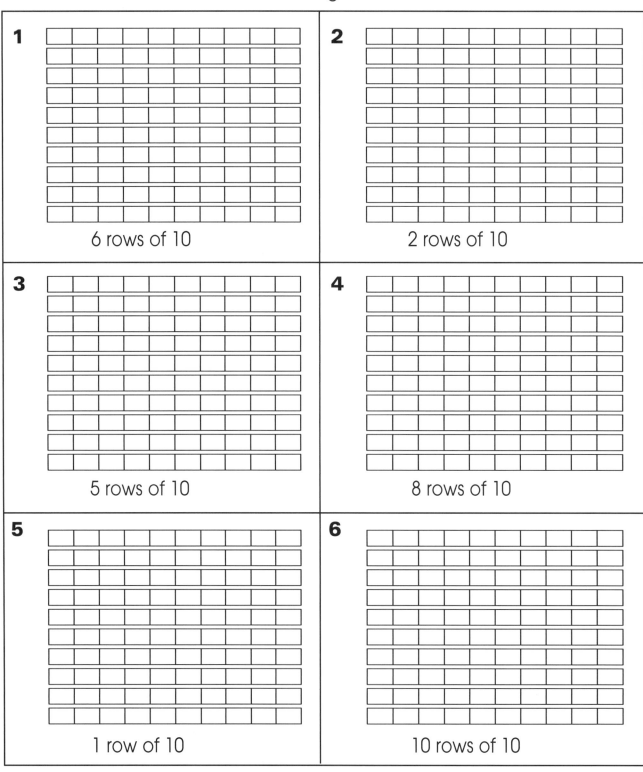

1

6 rows of 10

2

2 rows of 10

3

5 rows of 10

4

8 rows of 10

5

1 row of 10

6

10 rows of 10

How many rows of 10 in 30? ....

How many rows of 10 in 70? ....

Set 4: What a Lot of Points!

How many points on this star?

$1 \times 10 = 10$

---

1 How many points on 2 stars?

$2 \times 10 = \ldots\ldots\ldots$

---

2 How many points on 5 stars?

$5 \times 10 = \ldots\ldots\ldots$

---

3 How many points on 10 stars?

$10 \times 10 = \ldots\ldots\ldots$

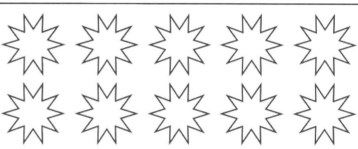

Did you count by 10s to get your answer? Or did you count every point?
Remember that counting by 10s is faster.

Finish these patterns.

4

5

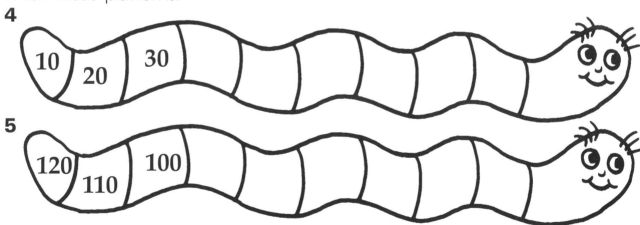

There are 30 points altogether. How many 10-pointed stars? ....

Set 5: What a Lot of Spots!

How many groups of 10 spots can you find?
Guess first. Check by circling the groups of 10.

1   My guess .... × 10

After counting .... × 10 = ...

2   My guess .... × 10

After counting .... × 10 = ...

3   My guess .... × 10

After counting .... × 10 = ...

4   My guess .... × 10

After counting .... × 10 = ...

Set 6: Draw Groups of 10

Draw your own pictures to match.
Write how many altogether.

1 3 bags with 10 smarties in each bag.

2 4 aliens with 10 legs each.

How many aliens if there are 70 legs altogether and each alien has 10 legs? ....

3 2 × 10 squares = ...

4 1 × 10 buttons = ...

I have 4 bags.
There are 10 jelly beans in each bag.
How many jelly beans do I have?

....

Set 7: Look for a Pattern

Colour in all the numbers as you count by 10.

1	2	3	4	5	6	7	8	9	10
11	12	13	14	15	16	17	18	19	20
21	22	23	24	25	26	27	28	29	30
31	32	33	34	35	36	37	38	39	40
41	42	43	44	45	46	47	48	49	50
51	52	53	54	55	56	57	58	59	60
61	62	63	64	65	66	67	68	69	70
71	72	73	74	75	76	77	78	79	80
81	82	83	84	85	86	87	88	89	90
91	92	93	94	95	96	97	98	99	100

1 What pattern can you see in the final digits?

....

2 What's the **first** number in this pattern?

....

3 What's the **sixth** number in this pattern?

....

4 Find the match. Draw a line to the egg that holds the answer.

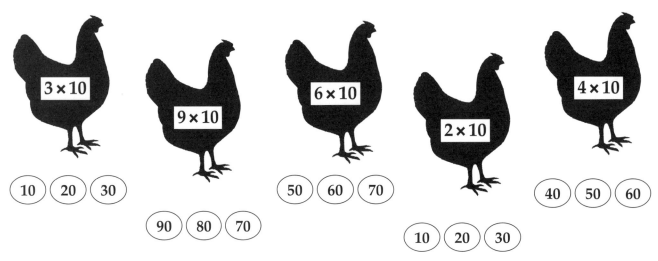

3×10

9×10

6×10

2×10

4×10

(10) (20) (30)

(90) (80) (70)

(50) (60) (70)

(10) (20) (30)

(40) (50) (60)

5 Circle the matching answer.

a 10×10	20	100	30
b 4×10	30	40	50
c 7×10	70	60	80
d 5×10	30	40	50

If my dog eats 10 small bones each day, how long will it take to eat 80 bones?

....

Set 8: Challenge

1 Time yourself to see how quickly you can find the answers.

a 4 × 10 = ... **b** 7 × 10 = ... **c** 1 × 10 = ... **d** 2 × 10 = ...

e 10 × 10 = ... **f** 5 × 10 = ... **g** 9 × 10 = ... **h** 3 × 10 = ...

Number of seconds ....

2 Fill in this grid as quickly as you can.

×	3	5	4	9	7	1	10	8	2	6
10										

Number of seconds ....

3 Do you remember your groups of 2?
Fill in this grid as quickly as you can.

×	4	8	3	10	6	2	5	9	7	1
10										
2										

Number of seconds ....

4 Try these number wheels.   Write the answers in the outer spaces.

a 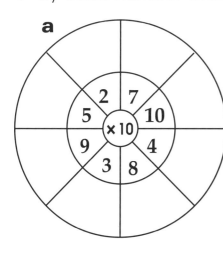 **b** 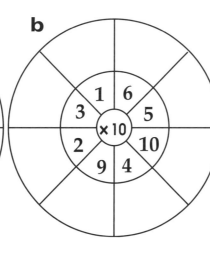 **c**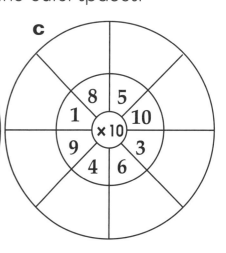

Set 9: Beat the Clock

Record your times in the graph at the bottom of the page.

1 Can you fill in this grid in less than 90 seconds?

×	5	2	10	1	4	6	8	7	9	3
10										

Number of seconds ....

2 Can you fill in this grid in less than 80 seconds?

×	10	3	7	4	5	2	9	1	6	8
10										

Number of seconds ....

3 Can you fill in this grid in less than 70 seconds?

×	2	9	6	3	8	10	7	4	1	5
10										

Number of seconds ....

4 Can you fill in this grid in less than 60 seconds?

×	3	8	1	10	2	4	5	9	7	6
10										

Number of seconds ....

My Time Graph

Grid 1										
Grid 2										
Grid 3										
Grid 4										
	10	20	30	40	50	60	70	80	90	100 or more

Number of seconds

Excel **Basic Skills** *Times Tables 1 Years 2–3* Unit 2

Set 10: Mind Munchers

Write the number sentence to match each story.

1 4 lunches at $10 each.
How much altogether?

………… × ………… = …………

2 3 rabbits with 10 baby
bunnies each. How many
bunnies?

………… × ………… = …………

3 7 trains with 10 carriages each.
How many carriages altogether?

………… × ………… = …………

4 6 trees with 10 pears each.
How many pears altogether?

………… × ………… = …………

Challenge

5 There are 90 fish.
Each tank has 10 fish.
How many tanks?

………… × ………… = …………

6 Each truck has 10 wheels.
I counted 50 wheels.
How many trucks?

………… × ………… = …………

7 Make up your own number story and write it here:

....

....

Write the number sentence for your story. ………… × ………… = …………

*There are 10 more people than
4 × 10. How many people
altogether?* ....

Set 11: Check-up

Before we move on to explore groups of 5, let's check
how much you remember about multiplying 2s and 10s.

1 How many groups?

$\boxed{}$ groups of $\boxed{}$

2 Draw a picture to match.

3 × 10

3 Draw a line to the correct answer.

10

$\boxed{5 \times 2}$

12

$\boxed{9 \times 10}$

$\boxed{6 \times 2}$

90

$\boxed{4 \times 10}$

40

4 Continue the counting patterns.

a 24 22 20 ....

b 100 90 80 ....

5 Do these in less than one minute.

a 4 × 2 = ...   **b** .... × 10 = 30 **c** 6 × .... = 12 **d** 5 × 10 = ...

e .... × 10 = 80 **f** 5 × .... = 10 **g** 7 × 10 = ...   **h** .... × 2 = 18

*There are 20 legs in the chook pen.
How many chooks are in the pen?*

....

Set 1: Groups of 5

Counting by 5s is also easy.
Perhaps it is because we have 5 fingers on each hand.
What do you think?

1 What else can you count that comes in fives?
(for example: sides on a pentagon, cents in a five-cent coin)

....

2 How many fingers on 1 hand?

5

.... set of .... fingers

5

3 How many toes on 2 feet?

5 + 5

.... sets of .... toes

4 How many sides on 3 pentagons?

.... + ... + ...

.... sets of .... sides

5 Can you see a pattern? ....

....

6 Write how you count by 5.

5   10   15   ....

*How many fingers and toes altogether
on four hands and two feet?*

....

Set 2: Rows of 5

You can sort things into equal rows of 5 to make a 5s array. The things line up in rows and columns. This is what 10 rows of 5 rabbits look like as an array.

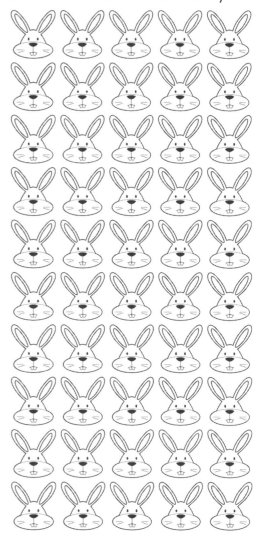

1 Draw 3 rows of 5 circles in an array.

2 Draw 5 rows of 5 triangles in an array.

3 Draw 7 rows of 5 rectangles in an array.

4 Draw 9 rows of 5 sticks in an array.

5 This is what 10 equal groups of 5 look like on a number line.

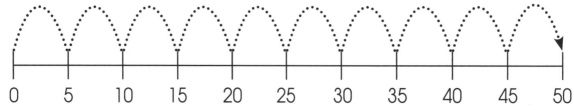

0   5   10   15   20   25   30   35   40   45   50

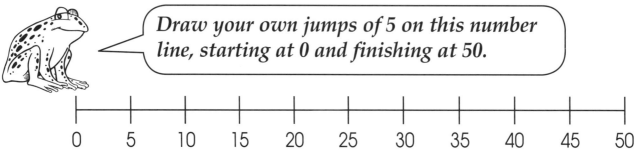

Draw your own jumps of 5 on this number line, starting at 0 and finishing at 50.

0   5   10   15   20   25   30   35   40   45   50

Set 3: Rows of 5

Colour in the rows to match.

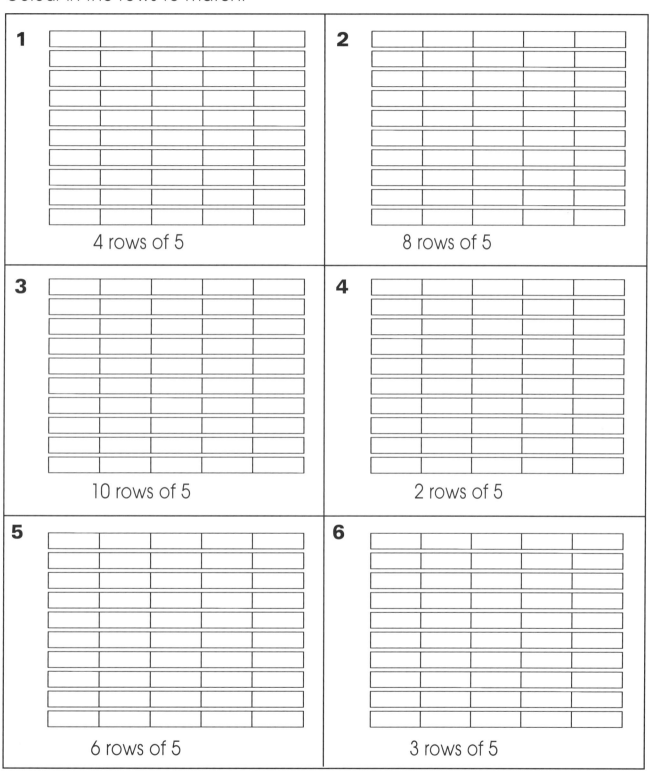

1

4 rows of 5

2

8 rows of 5

3

10 rows of 5

4

2 rows of 5

5

6 rows of 5

6

3 rows of 5

How many rows of 5 in 25? ....

How many rows of 5 in 35? ....

Set 4: Look for a Pattern

Colour in all the numbers as you count by 5s.

1	2	3	4	5	6	7	8	9	10
11	12	13	14	15	16	17	18	19	20
21	22	23	24	25	26	27	28	29	30
31	32	33	34	35	36	37	38	39	40
41	42	43	44	45	46	47	48	49	50
51	52	53	54	55	56	57	58	59	60
61	62	63	64	65	66	67	68	69	70
71	72	73	74	75	76	77	78	79	80
81	82	83	84	85	86	87	88	89	90
91	92	93	94	95	96	97	98	99	100

1 What pattern can you see in the final digits?

....

2 Look back at page 20. What do you notice?

....

....

Can you count forwards by 5s with your eyes shut? ....

What's the biggest number you can count to by 5s? ....

3 Fill in the missing numbers in these counting patterns.

a
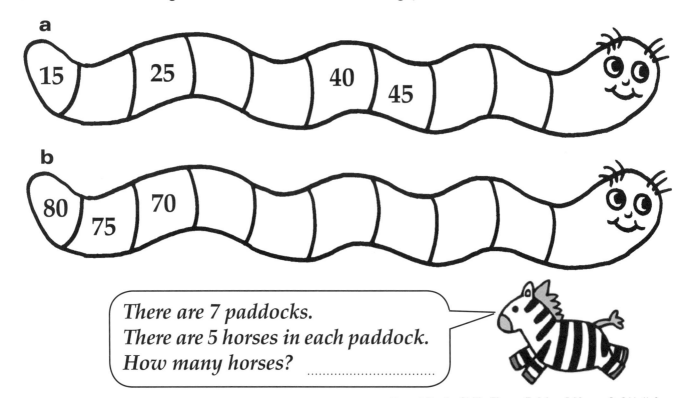
15   25   40 45

b
80 75 70

There are 7 paddocks.
There are 5 horses in each paddock.
How many horses? ....

Set 5: What a Lot of Arms!

1 How many arms on this starfish? ....

How many arms can you see in each picture?
Guess first. Check by counting. Use groups of 5 to help you count.

2

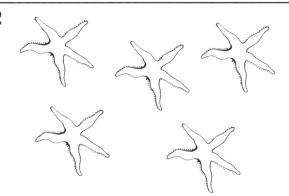

My guess .... arms

After counting .... × 5 = ...

3

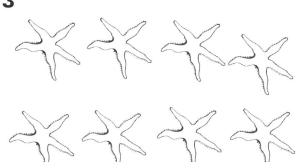

My guess .... arms

After counting .... × 5 = ...

4

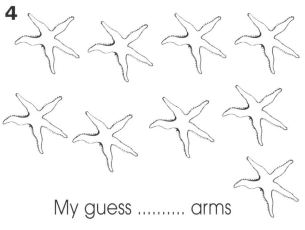

My guess .... arms

After counting .... × 5 = ...

5

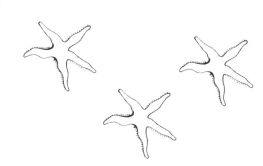

My guess .... arms

After counting .... × 5 = ...

6 Join the dots by adding 5s.

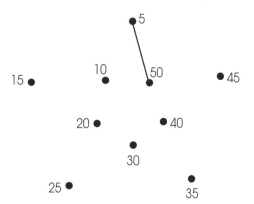

Set 6: *What a Lot of Spots!*

In games, you can throw a 5 like this. $1 \times$ = 5

What's your score if you throw three 5s? $3 \times$ = 15

Write in the missing numbers.

1 $6 \times$ = ...

2 $10 \times$ = ...

3 $2 \times$ = ...

4 $4 \times$ = ...

Did you get your answers counting by 5s?
Or did you count up all the spots?
Remember it's faster to count by 5s.

5 Try these.

    a $7 \times 5 =$ ....   **b** $1 \times 5 =$ ....   **c** $10 \times 5 =$ ....   **d** $2 \times 5 =$ ....

    e $5 \times 5 =$ ....   **f** $8 \times 5 =$ ....   **g** $3 \times 5 =$ ....   **h** $9 \times 5 =$ ....

6 Challenge.

    a .... $\times 5 = 35$ **b** .... $\times 5 = 5$

    c .... $\times 5 = 50$ **d** .... $\times 5 = 30$

    e .... $\times 5 = 25$ **f** .... $\times 5 = 40$

    g .... $\times 5 = 10$ **h** .... $\times 5 = 15$

My score is 20 and I only threw 5s. How many 5s did I throw?

....

Set 7: Draw Groups of 5

Draw your own pictures to match. Write the number sentences too.

1 3 boxes with 5 apples in each box.	**2** 6 faces with 5 freckles on each face.

3 Find the match.
Draw lines to the answers.

50   4 × 5   20   8 × 5   5 × 5

1 × 5   40   25   10 × 5   30

5   6 × 5

4 Finish these number wheels.

a
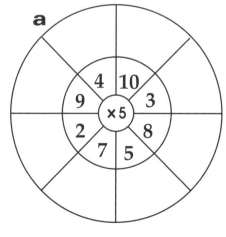

b
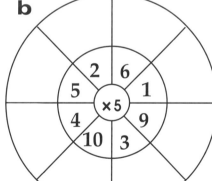

c
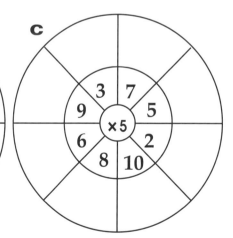

I have a brother and a sister, plus my mum and dad. Aunty Sue gave us $5 each. How much altogether?

....

Set 8: Riddles

1 Fill in the answers, then solve the riddles below using the code.

O: $6 \times 5 =$ .... I: $4 \times 5 =$ .... W: $10 \times 5 =$ .... R: $7 \times 5 =$ ....

M: $5 \times 5 =$ .... U: $9 \times 5 =$ .... C: $3 \times 5 =$ .... T: $8 \times 5 =$ ....

2 What is coming, but never arrives?

....
40   30   25   30   35   35   30   50

3 What did the girl say when she opened her piggy bank?

....
30   20   15   45   35   25   40

4 Time yourself to see how quickly you can find the answers.

a $9 \times 5 =$ .... **b** $6 \times 5 =$ .... **c** $3 \times 5 =$ .... **d** $2 \times 5 =$ ....

e $5 \times 5 =$ .... **f** $10 \times 5 =$ .... **g** $8 \times 5 =$ .... **h** $7 \times 5 =$ ....

Number of seconds ....

5 Do you remember your groups of 2 and 10 too?
Can you fill in this grid in less than 120 seconds?

	×	10	5	8	9	4	2	7	1	3	6
a	5										
b	10										
c	2										

Number of seconds ....

Set 9: Snail Patterns

Finish these snail patterns to show how you count forwards or backwards by 1s, 2s, 5s and 10s.

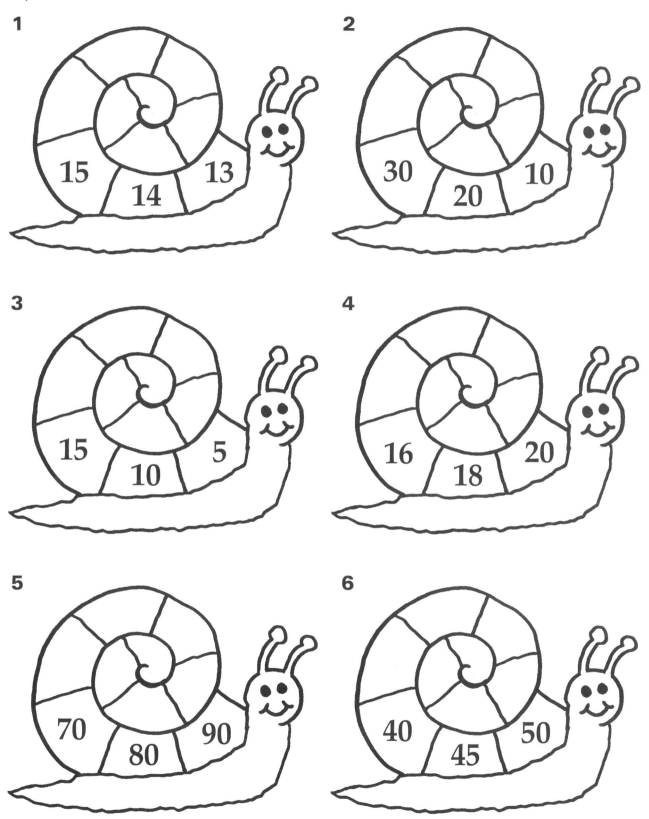

1 15 14 13

2 30 20 10

3 15 10 5

4 16 18 20

5 70 80 90

6 40 45 50

Set 10: Beat the Clock

Record your times on the graph at the bottom of the page.

1 Can you fill in this grid in less than 80 seconds?

×	10	5	3	2	7	9	6	4	8	1
5										

Number of seconds ....

2 Can you fill in this grid in less than 70 seconds?

×	4	1	9	5	10	3	8	7	2	6
5										

Number of seconds ....

3 Can you fill in this grid in less than 60 seconds?

×	2	7	1	9	5	8	6	10	4	3
5										

Number of seconds ....

4 Can you fill in this grid in less than 50 seconds?

×	3	8	1	5	0	4	9	7	6	2
5										

Number of seconds ....

My Time Graph

Grid 1										
Grid 2										
Grid 3										
Grid 4										
	10 or less	20	30	40	50	60	70	80	90	100 or more

Number of seconds

Set 11: Mind Munchers

Write the number sentence to match each story.

1 5 boxes with 5 books in each box. How many books altogether?

.... × .... = ...

2 7 cars with 5 people in each car. How many people altogether?

.... × .... = ...

3 2 cats with 5 mice each. How many mice altogether?

.... × .... = ...

4 4 socks with 5 holes in each sock. How many holes altogether?

.... × .... = ...

Challenge

5 Each squirrel has 5 nuts. There are 50 nuts altogether. How many squirrels?

.... × .... = ...

6 I save $5 each week. How many weeks will it take to save $30?

.... × .... = ...

7 Make up your own number story and write it here:

....

....

Write the number sentence for your story. .... × .... = ...

This lady loves poodles. She likes to put a pompom on each dog's leg and one on their tail. There are 20 pompoms. How many poodles?

....

Set 12: Check-up

Before we move on to explore doubling, let's check
how much you remember about multiplying by 2s, 5s and 10s.

1 How many groups?

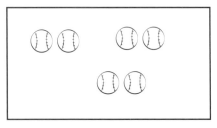 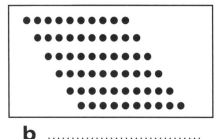 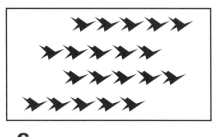

a .... **b** .... **c** ....

2 Draw a picture to match.

a 4 × 10   **b** 7 × 5   **c** 6 × 2

3 Match the number names by drawing a line.

70   3 × 2   18   8 × 10   80

7 × 10   25   5 × 5   6   9 × 2   50   10 × 5

4 Continue the counting patterns.

18 16 14 ....

90 80 70 ....

45 40 35 ....

5 Do these quickly.

a 4 × .... = 8   **b** .... × 2 = 20   **c** 8 × 2 = ...   **d** 3 × .... = 6

e .... × 5 = 20   **f** 10 × .... = 50   **g** .... × 5 = 40   **h** 3 × 5 = ...

 *Eight cakes cost $40. How much for 1 cake?* ....

UNIT 1: Groups of 2

Page 1 *Set 1: Groups of 2*
1 Answers will vary.
2 6, 2 + 2 + 2
3 8, 2 + 2 + 2 + 2, 4 groups of 2 wheels
4 10, 2 + 2 + 2 + 2 + 2, 5 groups of 2 eyes
Quick Question: There are 12 legs.

Page 2 *Set 2: Rows of 2*

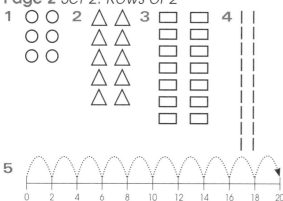

5

Page 3 *Set 3: Find the Groups of 2*
1 10, 5 groups of 2
2 6, 3 groups of 2
3 14, 7 groups of 2
4 8, 4 groups of 2
5 4, 2 groups of 2
6 10, 5 groups of 2

Page 4 *Set 4: What a Lot of Ears!*
1 8
2 12
3 18
4 20 groups of 2, 40 ears

Page 5 *Set 5: Counting by 2s*
1 a 0 2 4 6 8
   b 6 8 10 12 14
   c 10 12 14 16 18
   d 8 10 12 14 16
   e 16 18 20 22 24
2 20 18 16 14 12 10 8 6
3 Join 2 4 6 8 10 12 14 16 18 20 to make a fish.

Quick question: 30 28 26 24 22 20, 40 38 36 34 32 30, 50 48 46 44 42 40

Page 6 *Set 6: What a Lot of Socks!*
1 4, 2 groups of 2
2 6, 3 groups of 2
3 8, 4 groups of 2
4 10, 5 groups of 2
5 12, 6 groups of 2
6 14, 7 groups of 2
7 16, 8 groups of 2
8 18, 9 groups of 2
9 20, 10 groups of 2
10 e.g. The last digit repeats 0 2 4 6 8.
11 Answers will vary
Quick question: Answers will vary.

Page 7 *Set 7: What a Lot of Legs!*
The clowns have 12 legs.
Quick question: $4 \times 2 = 8$, $7 \times 2 = 14$

Page 8 *Set 8: Counting Balls*
1 12 balls, $6 \times 2 = 12$
2 10 balls, 5 groups of 2, $5 \times 2 = 10$
3

1	2	3	4	5	6	7	8	9	10
11	12	13	14	15	16	17	18	19	20
21	22	23	24	25	26	27	28	29	30
31	32	33	34	35	36	37	38	39	40
41	42	43	44	45	46	47	48	49	50
51	52	53	54	55	56	57	58	59	60
61	62	63	64	65	66	67	68	69	70
71	72	73	74	75	76	77	78	79	80
81	82	83	84	85	86	87	88	89	90
91	92	93	94	95	96	97	98	99	100

4 Answers will vary (e.g. the last digit goes in order 2 4 6 8 0).
5 8
6 20
Quick question: There are 9 groups of 2 balls in 18 balls.

Page 9 *Set 9: Mix and Match*
1 $9 \times 2 = 18$
2 $4 \times 2 = 8$
3 a 14 b 10 c 20 d 2
4 2 4 6 8 10 12 14 16 18 20
5 a 8 b 6 c 10 d 20 e 2 f 14
   g 18 h 12
Quick question: There is $8 altogether.

Page 10 *Set 10: Match Them Up*
1 $3 \times 2 = 6$, $6 \times 2 = 12$, $2 \times 2 = 4$
2 a 10 b 8 c 14 d 16
3 20 18 16 14 12 10 8 6 4 2
4 a 2 + 2 + 2 + 2 + 2 + 2 + 2, 7×2, 14
   b 2, 1 group of 2, 2
   c 2 + 2 + 2, 3 groups of 2, 3×2
   d 2 + 2 + 2 + 2 + 2, 5 groups of 2, 10
Quick question: There are 7 pairs.

Page 11 *Set 11: Challenge*
1 a 10 b 16 c 6 d 20 e 2 f 8 g 14 h 4
2 a 12 20 10 16 2 12 18 4 14 8

A1

b 6 16 2 14 20 4 12 10 8 18
c 20 2 8 16 6 12 14 18 4 10
Quick question: I bought 9 tins.

Page 12 *Set 12: Mind Munchers*
1 $10 \times 2 = 20$, $20
2 $5 \times 2 = 10$
3 $4 \times 2 = 8$
4 $3 \times 2 = 6$
5 $7 \times 2 = 14$ so there are 7 people.
6 $8 \times 2 = 16$ so there are 8 pairs.
7 Answers will vary.
Quick question: $10 \times 2 = 20$ so there are 10 big dogs.

Page 13 *Set 13: Check-up*
1 **a** 9 groups of 2 is 18 altogether.
  b 4 groups of 2 is 8 altogether.
2 **a** $6 \times 2 = 12$
  b $9 \times 2 = 18$
3 $7 \times 2 = 14$, $9 \times 2 = 18$, $6 \times 2 = 12$, $10 \times 2 = 20$, $3 \times 2 = 6$
4 **a** 8 10 12 14 16 18 20 22 24
  b 20 18 16 14 12 10 8 6 4
5 **a** 6 **b** 12 **c** 14 **d** 20 **e** 10
  f 16 **g** 8 **h** 2
Quick question: $8 \times 2 = 16$ so there are 8 children.

UNIT 2: Groups of 10

Page 14 *Set 1: Groups of 10*
1 Answers will vary (e.g. cents in a 10c coin, sides on a decagon).
2 1 group of 10
3 2 groups of 10, 20
4 3 groups of 10, 30
5 Answers will vary (e.g. the last digit is always 0).
6 10 20 30 40 50 60 70 80 90 100
Quick question: Each person has 2×10 fingers and toes. So 3 people have 6×10 or 60 fingers and toes.

Page 15 *Set 2: Rows of 10*
1 ☐☐☐☐☐☐☐☐☐☐
  ☐☐☐☐☐☐☐☐☐☐
2 ⬠⬠⬠⬠⬠⬠⬠⬠⬠⬠
  ⬠⬠⬠⬠⬠⬠⬠⬠⬠⬠
  ⬠⬠⬠⬠⬠⬠⬠⬠⬠⬠
  ⬠⬠⬠⬠⬠⬠⬠⬠⬠⬠

3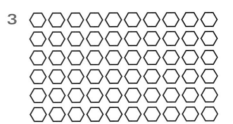

4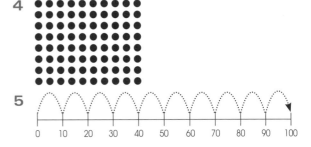

5

```
  ∩  ∩  ∩  ∩  ∩  ∩  ∩  ∩  ∩  ∩
0  10 20 30 40 50 60 70 80 90 100
```

Page 16 *Set 3: Rows of 10*
1 Colour any 6 rows of 10.
2 Colour any 2 rows of 10.
3 Colour any 5 rows of 10.
4 Colour any 8 rows of 10.
5 Colour just 1 row of 10.
6 Colour all 10 rows of 10.
Quick question: There are 3 rows of 10 in 30. There are 7 rows of 10 in 70.

Page 17 *Set 4: What a Lot of Points!*
1 20
2 50
3 100
4 10 20 30 40 50 60 70 80 90 100
5 120 110 100 90 80 70 60 50 40 30
Quick question: There are 3 10-pointed stars.

Page 18 *Set 5: What a Lot of Spots!*
Each guess will vary.
1 $3 \times 10 = 30$
2 $7 \times 10 = 70$
3 $5 \times 10 = 50$
4 $10 \times 10 = 100$

Page 19 *Set 6: Draw Groups of 10*
1 $3 \times 10 = 30$
2 $4 \times 10 = 40$
Quick question: There are 7 aliens.
3 $2 \times 10 = 20$
4 $1 \times 10 = 10$
Quick question: There are 40 jelly beans.

Page 20 Set 7: Look for a Pattern

1

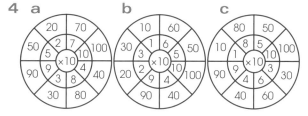

1	2	3	4	5	6	7	8	9	10
11	12	13	14	15	16	17	18	19	20
21	22	23	24	25	26	27	28	29	30
31	32	33	34	35	36	37	38	39	40
41	42	43	44	45	46	47	48	49	50
51	52	53	54	55	56	57	58	59	60
61	62	63	64	65	66	67	68	69	70
71	72	73	74	75	76	77	78	79	80
81	82	83	84	85	86	87	88	89	90
91	92	93	94	95	96	97	98	99	100

Answers will vary (e.g. the last digit is always 0, the tens digit goes in counting order from 1 to 10).

2 10

3 60

4 $3 \times 10 = 30$, $9 \times 10 = 90$, $6 \times 10 = 60$, $2 \times 10 = 20$, $4 \times 10 = 40$

5 **a** $10 \times 10 = 100$ **b** $4 \times 10 = 40$ **c** $7 \times 10 = 70$ **d** $5 \times 10 = 50$

Quick question: My dog will take 8 days to eat 80 small bones.

Page 21 Set 8: Challenge

1 **a** 40 **b** 70 **c** 10 **d** 20 **e** 100 **f** 50 **g** 90 **h** 30

2 30 50 40 90 70 10 100 80 20 60

3 **a** 40 80 30 100 60 20 50 90 70 10
   b 8 16 6 20 12 4 10 18 14 2

4 **a** **b** **c**

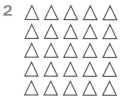

Page 22 Set 9: Beat the Clock

1 50 20 100 10 40 60 80 70 90 30

2 100 30 70 40 50 20 90 10 60 80

3 20 90 60 30 80 100 70 40 10 50

4 30 80 10 100 20 40 50 90 70 60

Page 23 Set 10: Mind Munchers

1 $4 \times 10 = 40$, $40

2 $3 \times 10 = 30$

3 $7 \times 10 = 70$

4 $6 \times 10 = 60$

5 $9 \times 10 = 90$ so there are 9 tanks.

6 $5 \times 10 = 50$ so there are 5 trucks.

7 Answers will vary.

Quick question: There are 50 people.

Page 24 Set 11: Check-up

1 4 groups of 10

2 Draw 30 objects

3 $5 \times 2 = 10$, $4 \times 10 = 40$, $6 \times 2 = 12$, $9 \times 10 = 90$

4 **a** 24 22 20 18 16 14 12 10
   b 100 90 80 70 60 50 40 30

5 **a** 8 **b** 3 **c** 2 **d** 50 **e** 8 **f** 2 **g** 70 **h** 9

Quick question: There are 10 chooks.

UNIT 3: Groups of 5

Page 25 Set 1: Groups of 5

1 Answers will vary (e.g. children in a quintuplet).

2 1 set of 5

3 2 sets of 5, 10

4 3 sets of 5, 15, 5 + 5 + 5

5 Answers will vary (e.g. the last digit is always 5 or 0).

6 5 10 15 20 25 30 35 40 45 50

Quick question: $6 \times 5 = 30$ so there are 30 fingers and toes altogether.

Page 26 Set 2: Rows of 5

1 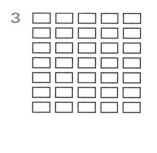 **2**

3 **4**

5

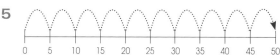

Page 27 Set 3: Rows of 5

1 Colour any 4 rows of 5.

2 Colour any 8 rows of 5.

3 Colour all 10 rows of 5.

4 Colour any 2 rows of 5.

5 Colour any 6 rows of 5.

6 Colour any 3 rows of 5.

Quick question: There are 5 rows of 5 in 25. There are 7 rows of 5 in 35.

Page 28 *Set 4: Look for a Pattern*

1

1	2	3	4	5	6	7	8	9	10
11	12	13	14	15	16	17	18	19	20
21	22	23	24	25	26	27	28	29	30
31	32	33	34	35	36	37	38	39	40
41	42	43	44	45	46	47	48	49	50
51	52	53	54	55	56	57	58	59	60
61	62	63	64	65	66	67	68	69	70
71	72	73	74	75	76	77	78	79	80
81	82	83	84	85	86	87	88	89	90
91	92	93	94	95	96	97	98	99	100

Answers will vary (e.g. if you keep counting by 5s to 100 the numbers form 2 columns headed by 5 and 10).

2 Answers will vary (e.g. the column on the right is exactly the same).

3 **a** 15 20 25 30 35 40 45 50 55 60
b 80 75 70 65 60 55 50 45 40 35

Quick question: There are 35 horses.

Page 29 *Set 5: What a Lot of Arms!*

1 5
2 5 × 5 = 25
3 8 × 5 = 40
4 9 × 5 = 45
5 3 × 5 = 15
6 Join the dots: Count by 5 and join 5 10 15 20 25 30 35 40 45 50 to create a star. Join 5 10 15 20 25 to create another star.

Page 30 *Set 6: What a Lot of Spots!*

1 6 × 5 = 30
2 10 × 5 = 50
3 2 × 5 = 10
4 4 × 5 = 20
5 **a** 35 **b** 5 **c** 50 **d** 10 **e** 25 **f** 40 **g** 15 **h** 45
6 **a** 7 **b** 1 **c** 10 **d** 6 **e** 5 **f** 8 **g** 2 **h** 3

Quick question: I threw four 5s.

Page 31 *Set 7: Draw Groups of 5*

1 3 × 5 = 15
2 6 × 5 = 30
3 4 × 5 = 20, 8 × 5 = 40, 5 × 5 = 25, 1 × 5 = 5, 6 × 5 = 30, 10 × 5 = 50

4 **a**   **b**   **c**

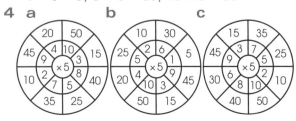

Quick question: Aunty Sue gave my family $20.

Page 32 *Set 8: Riddles*

1 C = 15, I = 20, M = 25, O = 30, R = 35, T = 40, U = 45, W = 50
2 TOMORROW
3 OICURMT (Oh I see you are empty)
4 **a** 45 **b** 30 **c** 15 **d** 10 **e** 25 **f** 50 **g** 40 **h** 35
5 × 5: 50 25 40 45 20 10 35 5 15 30
× 10: 100 50 80 90 40 20 70 10 30 60
× 2: 20 10 16 18 8 4 14 2 6 12

Page 33 *Set 9: Snail Patterns*

1 13 14 15 16 17 18 19 20 21 22
2 10 20 30 40 50 60 70 80 90 100
3 5 10 15 20 25 30 35 40 45 50
4 20 18 16 14 12 10 8 6 4 2
5 90 80 70 60 50 40 30 20 10 0
6 50 45 40 35 30 25 20 15 10 5

Page 34 *Set 10: Beat the Clock*

1 50 25 15 10 35 45 30 20 40 5
2 20 5 45 25 50 15 40 35 10 30
3 10 35 5 45 25 40 30 50 20 15
4 15 40 5 25 0 20 45 35 30 10

Page 35 *Set 11: Mind Munchers*

1 5 × 5 = 25
2 7 × 5 = 35
3 2 × 5 = 10
4 4 × 5 = 20
5 10 × 5 = 50 so there are 10 squirrels.
6 6 × 5 = 30 so it will take 6 weeks.
7 Answers will vary.

Quick question: She has 4 poodles.

Page 36 *Set 12: Check-up*

1 **a** 3 groups of 2
  b 6 groups of 10
  c 4 groups of 5
2 **a** Draw 40 objects
  b Draw 35 objects
  c Draw 12 objects
3 3 × 2 = 6, 7 × 10 = 70, 5 × 5 = 25, 9 × 2 = 18, 8 × 10 = 80, 10 × 5 = 50
4 **a** 18 16 14 12 10 8 6 4 2
  b 90 80 70 60 50 40 30 20 10
  c 45 40 35 30 25 20 15 10 5
5 **a** 2 **b** 10 **c** 16 **d** 2 **e** 4 **f** 5 **g** 8 **h** 15

Quick question: One cake costs $5.

UNIT 4: Doubling

Page 37 *Set 1: Doubling*
1 10 friends
2 4 frogs
3 20 toys
4 6 books
5 14
6 Double 4, $2 \times 4 = 8$
7 Double 9, $2 \times 9 = 18$
8 Double 10, $2 \times 10 = 20$
9 Double 5, $2 \times 5 = 10$
Quick question: I have 8 fish.

Page 38 *Set 2: Look for a Pattern*
1 6
2 8
3 10
4 12
5

1	2	3	4	5	6	7	8	9	10
11	12	13	14	15	16	17	18	19	20
21	22	23	24	25	26	27	28	29	30
31	32	33	34	35	36	37	38	39	40
41	42	43	44	45	46	47	48	49	50
51	52	53	54	55	56	57	58	59	60
61	62	63	64	65	66	67	68	69	70
71	72	73	74	75	76	77	78	79	80
81	82	83	84	85	86	87	88	89	90
91	92	93	94	95	96	97	98	99	100

Answers will vary (e.g. it is the same as counting by 2s , you never colour in odd numbers).
6 2
7 16
8 Answers will vary (e.g. it is exactly the same pattern as for groups of 2).
Quick question: There are 8 legs on half this alien.

Page 39 *Set 3: Seeing Double*
1 **a** Draw 10 more circles, $2 \times 10 = 20$
   b Draw 5 more stars, $2 \times 5 = 10$
2 Answers will vary.
3 **a** $2 \times 3 = 6$ **b** Draw 1 spot, $2 \times 1 = 2$
   c Draw 2 spots, $2 \times 2 = 4$
   d Draw 5 spots, $2 \times 5 = 10$
   e Draw 4 spots, $2 \times 4 = 8$
   f Draw 6 spots, $2 \times 6 = 12$
Quick question: Your score is 14.

Page 40 *Set 4: Draw Double*
1 **a** Draw 20 crosses, $2 \times 10 = 20$
   b Draw 16 sticks, $2 \times 8 = 16$
Quick question: I am 16.

2 Double 5 is 10, Twice 7 is 14, Double 8 is 16, Two times 3 is 6, Two times 2 is 4, Twice 10 is 20.
3

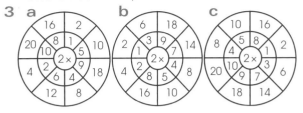

Quick question: I am 20.

Page 41 *Set 5: Riddles*
1 A = 4, C = 6, E = 8, K = 12, H = 10, R = 14, S = 16, T = 18, Y = 20
2 Because THEY'RE CRACKERS.
3 **a** 6 **b** 20 **c** 10 **d** 2 **e** 16 **f** 8 **g** 12 **h** 18
4 **a** 3 **b** 2 **c** 5 **d** 1 **e** 16 **f** 2 **g** 12 **h** 2
5 14 8 20 4 18 12 16 10 6 2
Quick question: 30 cents.

Page 42 *Set 6: Mind Munchers*
1 $2 \times 4 = 8$
2 $2 \times 10 = 20$
3 $2 \times 7 = 14$
4 $2 \times 3 = 6$
5 $2 \times 5 = 10$ so it will take me 2 weeks.
6 $2 \times 6 = 12$ so there are 6 children.
7 Answers will vary.
Quick question: There are 2 snakes.

Page 43 *Set 7: Beat the Clock*
1 6 14 4 18 8 20 2 10 12 16
2 10 20 2 12 8 18 4 14 16 6
3 2 14 20 8 16 6 10 4 12 18
4 8 18 4 10 20 16 6 12 2 14

Page 44 *Set 8: Check-up*
1 **a** 2 groups of 4 = 8
   b 6 groups of 2 = 12
2 **a** Draw 8 objects   **b** Draw 40 objects
3 $9 \times 10 = 90$, $3 \times 5 = 15$, $2 \times 8 = 16$, $9 \times 2 = 18$
4 **a** 10 12 14 16 18 20 22 24
   b 90 80 70 60 50 40 30 20
   c 65 60 55 50 45 40 35 30
   d 26 24 22 20 18 16 14 12
5 **a** 10 **b** 5 **c** 7 **d** 2 **e** 3 **f** 2 **g** 40 **h** 2

UNIT 5: Groups of 1

Page 45 *Set 1: Groups of 1*
1 **a** $3 \times 1 = 3$ **b** $6 \times 1 = 6$
Quick question: $8 \times 1 = 8$

2

1	2	3	4	5	6	7	8	9	10
11	12	13	14	15	16	17	18	19	20
21	22	23	24	25	26	27	28	29	30
31	32	33	34	35	36	37	38	39	40
41	42	43	44	45	46	47	48	49	50
51	52	53	54	55	56	57	58	59	60
61	62	63	64	65	66	67	68	69	70
71	72	73	74	75	76	77	78	79	80
81	82	83	84	85	86	87	88	89	90
91	92	93	94	95	96	97	98	99	100

Answers will vary (e.g. it is just all the numbers from 1 onwards in counting order).

3 1

4 10

5 20

Page 46 *Set 2: Rows of 1*

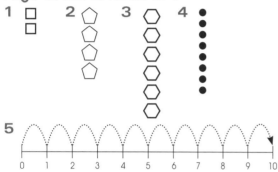

5

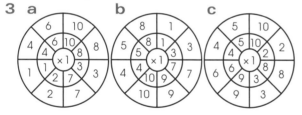

Page 47 *Set 3: Draw Groups of 1*

1 **a** Draw 2 bananas altogether.
b Draw 3 cats altogether.

2 $5 \times 1 = 5$, $4 \times 1 = 4$, $9 \times 1 = 9$, $8 \times 1 = 8$, $2 \times 1 = 2$, $3 \times 1 = 3$

3 **a**   **b**   **c**

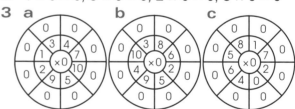

Quick question: I am 8.

Page 48 *Set 4: Riddles*

1 A = 8, C = 9, D = 4, I = 2, L = 3, N = 6, O = 5, S = 10, T = 7

2 ON A TOADSTOOL

3 IC (icy)

4 **a** 3 **b** 6 **c** 10 **d** 5 **e** 8 **f** 2 **g** 4 **h** 7

5 **a** 3 **b** 4 **c** 7 **d** 5 **e** 1 **f** 2 **g** 1 **h** 1

Quick question: I am 19.

Page 49 *Set 5: Mind Munchers*

1 **a** $6 \times 1 = 6$
b $4 \times 1 = 4$

2 3 7 2 9 4 10 1 5 6 8

3 4 9 1 7 3 5 2 8 6 10

4 5 10 3 8 1 4 9 6 2 7

Page 50 *Set 6: Check-up*

1 **a** 3 groups of 5 = 15
b 2 groups of 8 = 16
c 6 groups of 2 = 12
d 4 groups of 10 = 40

2 **a** $9 \times 1 = 9$ **b** $5 \times 10 = 50$
c $2 \times 5 = 10$ **d** $2 \times 4 = 8$
e $9 \times 2 = 18$ **f** $4 \times 10 = 40$

3 **a** 37 36 35 34 33 32 31 30
b 30 28 26 24 22 20 18 16
c 120 110 100 90 80 70 60
d 85 80 75 70 65 60 55 50

4 **a** 10 **b** 7 **c** 9 **d** 5 **e** 6 **f** 20
g 8 **h** 2

UNIT 6: Groups of 0

Page 51 *Set 1: Groups of 0*

1 **a** $3 \times 0 = 0$ **b** $4 \times 0 = 0$

2 The answers are always 0.

3

1	2	3	4	5	6	7	8	9	10
11	12	13	14	15	16	17	18	19	20
21	22	23	24	25	26	27	28	29	30
31	32	33	34	35	36	37	38	39	40
41	42	43	44	45	46	47	48	49	50
51	52	53	54	55	56	57	58	59	60
61	62	63	64	65	66	67	68	69	70
71	72	73	74	75	76	77	78	79	80
81	82	83	84	85	86	87	88	89	90
91	92	93	94	95	96	97	98	99	100

4 There is no pattern as you don't colour in anything!

Quick question: $10 \times 0 = 0$

Page 52 *Set 2: Draw Groups of 0*

1 **a** $4 \times 0 = 0$ **b** $2 \times 0 = 0$

2 $4 \times 0 = 0$, $5 \times 0 = 0$, $2 \times 0 = 0$, $3 \times 0 = 0$

3 **a**   **b**   **c**

4 **a** 0 **b** 0 **c** 0 **d** 0 **e** 0 **f** 0

Quick question: I am 0.

Page 53 *Set 3: Mind Munchers*

1 **a** $7 \times 0 = 0$ **b** $5 \times 0 = 0$

2 0 0 0 0 0 0 0 0 0 0

3 0 0 0 0 0 0 0 0 0 0

Page 54 *Set 4: Check-up*

1 **a** $8 \times 1 = 8$ **b** $2 \times 6 = 12$ **c** $10 \times 2 = 20$
d $8 \times 5 = 40$ **e** $7 \times 10 = 70$ **f** $10 \times 0 = 0$

2 **a** 30 28 26 24 22 20 18 16 14 12

b 120 110 100 90 80 70 60 50 40 30

c 55 50 45 40 35 30 25 20 15 10

3 a 10 **b** 4 **c** 2 **d** 0 **e** 9 **f** 5 **g** 70 **h** 5

4 a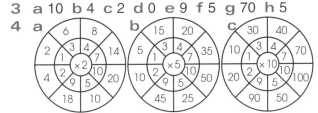

UNIT 7: Groups of 3

Page 55 *Set 1: Groups of 3*

1 1 group of 3, 3

2 2 groups of 3, 6

3 3 groups of 3, 9, 3 + 3 + 3

4 4 groups of 3, 12, 3 + 3 + 3 + 3

5 6 groups of 3 dots = 18 dots

6 3 6 9 12 15 18 21 24 27 30

Quick question: There are 8 children altogether.

Page 56 *Set 2: Rows of 3*

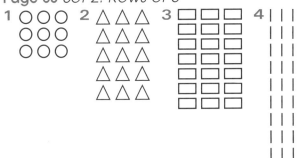

5

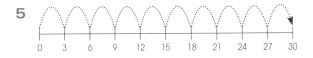

Page 57 *Set 3: More About 3*

1 6 × 3 = 18

2 3 × 3 = 9

3

1	2	3	4	5	6	7	8	9	10
11	12	13	14	15	16	17	18	19	20
21	22	23	24	25	26	27	28	29	30
31	32	33	34	35	36	37	38	39	40
41	42	43	44	45	46	47	48	49	50
51	52	53	54	55	56	57	58	59	60
61	62	63	64	65	66	67	68	69	70
71	72	73	74	75	76	77	78	79	80
81	82	83	84	85	86	87	88	89	90
91	92	93	94	95	96	97	98	99	100

The final digits go 3 6 9, then 2 5 8, then 1 4 7 0.

Quick question: Answers will vary.

4 18 15 12 9

5 30 27 24 21 18

6 a 3 6 9 12 15 18 21 24 27 30

b 30 27 24 21 18 15 12 9 6 3

Page 58 *Set 4: What a Lot of Dragons!*

1 3 × 3 = 9

2 8 × 3 = 24

3 Draw 15 marbles altogether, 5 × 3 = 15.

4 Join 0 3 6 9 12 15 18 21 24 27 30 to create a house with a chimney.

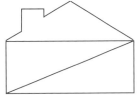

Quick question: 7 mangoes cost $21.

Page 59 *Set 5: Find the Match*

1 4 × 3 = 12, 8 × 3 = 24, 5 × 3 = 15, 1 × 3 = 3, 6 × 3 = 18, 10 × 3 = 30

2 A = 12, C = 27, N = 24, O = 21, P = 6, S = 15, T = 9, U = 18.

3 AN OCTOPUSS

4 a 27 **b** 18 **c** 9 **d** 21 **e** 15 **f** 30 **g** 24 **h** 6

5 12 21 9 3 6 15 24 18 27 30

Page 60 *Set 6: Beat the Clock*

1 18 3 27 12 21 6 10 9 30 24

2 30 15 9 6 21 27 18 12 24 3

3 6 21 3 27 15 24 18 30 12 9

4 12 21 0 9 24 15 6 27 3 18

Page 61 *Set 7: Mind Munchers*

1 4 × 3 = 12

2 9 × 3 = 27

3 6 × 3 = 18

4 7 × $3 = $21

5 10 × 3 = 30 so there are 10 squirrels.

6 5 × 3 = 15 so there are 5 flowers.

7 Answers will vary.

Page 62 *Set 8: Check-up*

1 Draw 18 objects.

2 Draw 0 objects.

3 7 × 3 = 21, 3 × 5 = 15, 2 × 7 = 14, 7 × 10 = 70, 5 × 5 = 25, 9 × 0 = 0

4 a   **b**   **c**

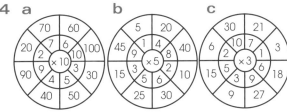

5 a 8 **b** 3 **c** 5 **d** 0 **e** 3 **f** 10 **g** 1 **h** 2

Quick question: 1 cake costs $3.

UNIT 8: Groups of 4

Page 63 *Set 1: Groups of 4*
1 Answers will vary (e.g. wheels on a car, rowers in a quad ...).
2 8 legs
3 12 legs
4 16 sides
5 20 wheels
6 **a** 6 groups of 4, 6 × 4 = 24
   b 7 groups of 4, 7 × 4 = 28
7 4 8 12 16 20 24 28 32 36 40
Quick question: There are 14 legs altogether (if the table and chair each have 4 legs).

Page 64 *Set 2: Rows of 4*

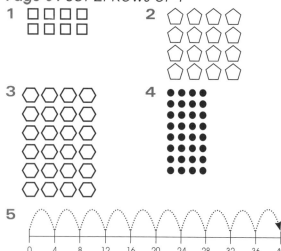

Page 65 *Set 3: Look for a Pattern*
1

1	2	3	4	5	6	7	8	9	10
11	12	13	14	15	16	17	18	19	20
21	22	23	24	25	26	27	28	29	30
31	32	33	34	35	36	37	38	39	40
41	42	43	44	45	46	47	48	49	50
51	52	53	54	55	56	57	58	59	60
61	62	63	64	65	66	67	68	69	70
71	72	73	74	75	76	77	78	79	80
81	82	83	84	85	86	87	88	89	90
91	92	93	94	95	96	97	98	99	100

Answers will vary (e.g. if you continue colouring to 100 then the numbers are in columns missing every second number). The final digit always ends in 4, 8, 2, 6 then 0.
2 8
3 32
4 40
5 **a** 16 **b** 28 **c** 4 **d** 8 **e** 32 **f** 40
   g 20 **h** 36

6

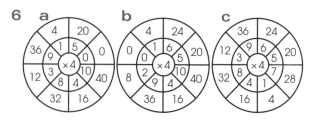

Page 66 *Set 4: Beat the Clock*
1 20 8 40 4 16 24 32 28 0 36
2 40 12 28 16 0 20 8 36 4 24
3 8 36 0 24 12 32 40 28 16 4
4 36 0 32 4 40 8 16 20 12 28

Page 67 *Set 5: Mind Munchers*
1 3 × 4 = 12
2 10 × $4 = $40
3 7 × 4 = 28
4 5 × 4 = 20
5 9 × 4 = 36 so there must be 9 squares.
6 5 × 4 = 20 so there must be 5 cars.
7 Answers will vary.
Quick question: 12–15 postmen have visited.

Page 68 *Set 6: Check-up*
1

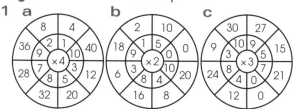

2 **a** 18 **b** 6 **c** 0 **d** 36 **e** 2 **f** 9 **g** 2 **h** 70
3 **a** 36 32 4 40 8 16 20 12 28 24
   b 21 15 0 30 24 12 6 9 3 27
   c 15 40 5 50 10 20 25 45 35 30
   d 80 10 100 30 0 20 90 40 70 60

Set 1: Doubling

'Double a number' means the same as 'two times' or 'twice as many'.

1 I have 5 friends. You have twice as many. How many friends do you have? 2 × 5 = ...	**2** I have 2 frogs. You have double. How many frogs do you have? 2 × 2 = ...
3 I have 10 toys. You have two times that. How many toys do you have? 2 × 10 = ...	**4** I have 3 books. You have double that number. How many books do you have? 2 × 3 = ...

What a lot of spots!
This ladybird has spots on both wings. How many spots can you see?

5    Double 7

2 × 7 = ...

Write the number of spots for these ladybirds.

6    Double ....

2 × .... = ...

7    Double ....

2 × .... = ...

8    Double ....

2 × .... = ...

9 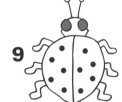   Double ....

2 × .... = ...

 You have 16 fish. You have twice as many fish as I have. How many fish do I have? ....

Set 2: *Look for a Pattern*

These aliens are missing half their body.
Draw in the other half of each alien.   Write how many legs altogether.

1 2 × 3 = ...

2 2 × 4 = ...

3 2 × 5 = ...

4 2 × 6 = ...

1	2	3	4	5	6	7	8	9	10
11	12	13	14	15	16	17	18	19	20
21	22	23	24	25	26	27	28	29	30
31	32	33	34	35	36	37	38	39	40
41	42	43	44	45	46	47	48	49	50
51	52	53	54	55	56	57	58	59	60
61	62	63	64	65	66	67	68	69	70
71	72	73	74	75	76	77	78	79	80
81	82	83	84	85	86	87	88	89	90
91	92	93	94	95	96	97	98	99	100

5 Colour in the number that
is double the numbers
from 1 to 10. What pattern can
you see in the final digits?

....

....

Can you continue doubling?

....

6 What's the first
number in this pattern? ....

7 What's the eighth
number in this pattern? ....

8 Look back at page 8.
What do you notice?

....

....

*An alien has 18 legs.
How many legs on
half an alien?* ....

Set 3: Seeing Double

1 Under each picture, repeat the pattern.
Write a number sentence to match the picture.

a 2 × 10 = ...

b 2 × 5 = ...

2 Double it. Throw a die eight times.
For each throw write down double the number as a number sentence.

For example   2 × 5 = 10

a .... **b** .... **c** .... **d** ....

e .... **f** .... **g** .... **h** ....

Can you double the number in your head?

3 Draw the other die and finish the number sentence.

a
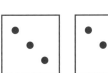

2 × 3 = ...

b
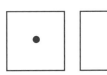

2 × 1 = ...

c
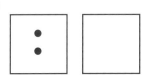

2 × 2 = ...

d

2 × .... = ...

e

2 × .... = ...

f
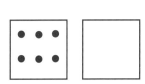

2 × .... = ...

My score is 7.
You threw double this.
What's your score? ....

Set 4: Draw Double

1 Draw your own pictures and write number sentences to match.

a 2 groups of 10 crosses	**b** 2 rows of 8 sticks

2 Find the match.
Draw lines to match the number names.

Double 5   16   Double 8

10   14

Two times 3   Twice 10   4

6

Two times 2   Twice 7

20

I am double 4 then double that again. What number am I?

....

3 Finish these number wheels.

a 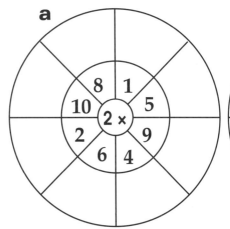   **b** 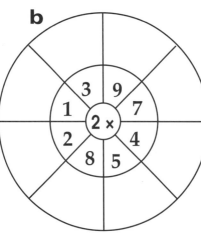   **c**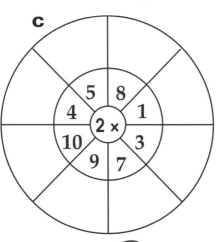

I am double 5 then double that again. What number am I?

....

Set 5: Riddles

1 Find the answers then solve the riddle below using the code.

A: 2 × 2 =.......... R: 2 × 7 =.......... K: 2 × 6 =.......... E: 2 × 4 =.......... Y: 2 × 10..........

H: 2 × 5 =.......... S: 2 × 8 =.......... C: 2 × 3 =.......... T: 2 × 9 =..........

2 Why do idiots eat biscuits?

Because ....' ....'
       18 10 8 20 14 8   6 14 4 6 12 8 14 16

3 Time yourself to see how quickly you can find the answers.

a 2 × 3 =.......... **b** 2 × 10 =.......... **c** 2 × 5 =.......... **d** 2 × 1 =..........

e 2 × 8 =.......... **f** 2 × 4 =.......... **g** 2 × 6 =.......... **h** 2 × 9 =..........

Number of seconds ....

4 Challenge

a 2 × .... = 6 **b** .... × 10 = 20 **c** 2 × .... = 10 **d** 2 × .... = 2

e 2 × 8 = ... **f** 2 × .... = 4 **g** 2 × 6 = ... **h** .... × 9 = 18

Number of seconds ....

5 Can you do this grid just using your head?

×	7	4	10	2	9	6	8	5	3	1
2										

Licorice straps are 10 cents each.
Musk sticks are 5 cents.
How much for 2 licorice straps and
2 musk sticks? ....

Set 6: Mind Munchers

Write the number sentence to match each story.

1 Two possums with
4 babies each.
How many babies?

.... × .... = ...

2 Two houses with 10 people in
each house.
How many people?

.... × .... = ...

3 Two fish eat 7 worms each.
How many worms?

.... × .... = ...

4 Two cars with 3 people
in each.
How many people?

.... × .... = ...

Challenge

5 I get $5 pocket money
each week.   How long will it
take me to get $10?

.... × .... = ...

6 I can see 12 little legs.
How many children?

.... × .... = ...

7 Make up your own number story and write it here.

....

....

Write the number sentence for your story.   .... × .... = ...

Each snake has 9 stripes.
There are 18 stripes altogether.
How many snakes are there? ....

Set 7: Beat the Clock

Record your times on the graph at the bottom of the page.

1 Can you fill in this grid in less than 80 seconds?

×	3	7	2	9	4	10	1	5	6	8
2										

Number of seconds ....

2 Can you fill in this grid in less than 70 seconds?

×	5	10	1	6	4	9	2	7	8	3
2										

Number of seconds ....

3 Can you fill in this grid in less than 60 seconds?

×	1	7	10	4	8	3	5	2	6	9
2										

Number of seconds ....

4 Can you fill in this grid in less than 50 seconds?

×	4	9	2	5	10	8	3	6	1	7
2										

Number of seconds ....

My Time Graph

	10 or less	20	30	40	50	60	70	80	90	100 or more
Grid 1										
Grid 2										
Grid 3										
Grid 4										

Number of seconds

Set 8: Check-up

Before we move on to explore groups of 1, let's check
how much you remember about multiplying by 2, 5, 10
and doubling.

1 How many objects?

a 2 groups of 4 = ...

b .... groups of .... = ...

2 Draw a picture to match.

a 2 × 4 = ...

b 4 × 10 = ...

3 Draw a line to the correct answer.

9 × 10   90   16   9 × 2

18   3 × 5   2 × 8   15

4 Continue the counting patterns.

a 10   12   14   ....

b 90   80   70   ....

c 65   60   55   ....

d 26   24   22   ....

5 Do these quickly.

a 2 × 5 = ...   **b** .... × 10 = 50   **c** 2 × .... = 14   **d** .... × 6 = 12

e .... × 2 = 6   **f** 6 × .... = 12   **g** 8 × 5 = ...   **h** 3 × .... = 6

Set 1: Groups of 1

Imagine you are at the aquarium and you see a seahorse.

1 group of 1 seahorse   1 x 1 = 1

You look carefully again. This time you see one seahorse near a rock and another seahorse by some weeds.

2 groups of 1 seahorse   2 x 1 = 2

1 Write the number sentence to match the following:

a 3 seahorses .... x .... = ...   **b** 6 seahorses .... x .... = ...

You look carefully. You see 8 different seahorses. Write the number sentence to match.

....

2 Colour in each answer as you multiply from 1 x 1 to 10 x 1.

What pattern can you see in the final digits? ....

1	2	3	4	5	6	7	8	9	10
11	12	13	14	15	16	17	18	19	20
21	22	23	24	25	26	27	28	29	30
31	32	33	34	35	36	37	38	39	40
41	42	43	44	45	46	47	48	49	50
51	52	53	54	55	56	57	58	59	60
61	62	63	64	65	66	67	68	69	70
71	72	73	74	75	76	77	78	79	80
81	82	83	84	85	86	87	88	89	90
91	92	93	94	95	96	97	98	99	100

3 What's the first number in this pattern?

....

4 What's the tenth number in this pattern?

....

5 What will be the twentieth number in this pattern?

....

Set 2: Groups of 1

You can sort things into equal rows of 1. This makes a 1s array. The things line up in rows and 1 column. This is what 10 rows of 1 shoe look like as an array.

1 Draw 2 rows of 1 square as an array.	**2** Draw 4 rows of 1 pentagon as an array.
3 Draw 6 rows of 1 hexagon as an array.	**4** Draw 8 rows of 1 dot as an array.

5 This is what 10 equal groups of 1 look like on a number line.

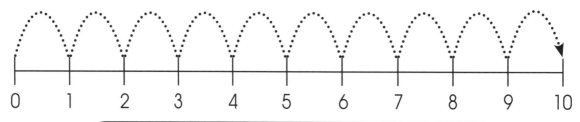

Draw your own jumps of 1 on this number line, starting at 0 and finishing at 10.

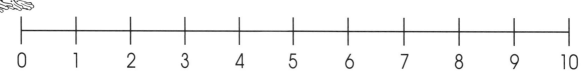

Set 3: Draw Groups of 1

Drawing groups of 'one' is easy.
You just draw one thing each time.

For example,
4 groups of 1

$4 \times 1 = 4$

1 Draw your own pictures to match these stories.

a 2 plates with 1 banana on each plate	**b** 3 boxes with a cat in each box

2 Find the match.
Draw lines to show the match.

2   9 9×1 3

8   4 4×1 2×1 3×1

5×1 8×1 5

3 Finish these number wheels.

a

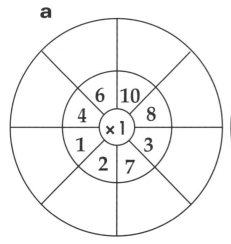

b

c

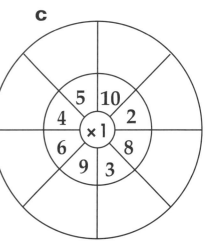

*I am 3 groups of one, plus 5 groups of one.
What number am I?* ....

Set 4: Riddles

Find the answers then solve the riddles below using the code.

1 A: 8 x 1 = ...   I: 2 x 1 = ...   C: 9 x 1 = ...   O: 5 x 1 = ...

N: 6 x 1 = ...   S: 10 x 1 = ...   D: 4 x 1 = ...   T: 7 x 1 = ...

L: 3 x 1 = ...

2 Where do frogs sit?

....
  5   6   8   7   5   8   4   10   7   5   5   3

3 How can you spell cold with only two letters?

....
  2   9

4 Time yourself to see how quickly you can find these answers.
Can you do this just using your head?

  a 3 x 1 = ...   **b** 6 x 1 = ...   **c** 10 x 1 = ...   **d** 5 x 1 = ...

  e 8 x 1 = ...   **f** 2 x 1 = ...   **g** 4 x 1 = ...   **h** 7 x 1 = ...

Number of seconds ....

5 Challenge

  a .... x 1 = 3   **b** 4 x 1 = ...   **c** .... x 1 = 7   **d** .... x 1 = 5

  e 9 x .... = 9   **f** .... x 1 = 2   **g** 10 x .... = 10 **h** 1 x .... = 1

Number of seconds ....

I am ten more than 9 groups of one.
What number am I? ....

Set 5: Mind Munchers

1 Write the number sentence to match each story:

a 6 boxes with 1 present in each box. How many presents?	**b** 4 horses with 1 rider on each horse. How many riders?
.... × .... = ...	.... × .... = ...

Beat the clock.

2 Can you fill in this grid in less than 70 seconds?

×	3	7	2	9	4	10	1	5	6	8
1										

Number of seconds ....

3 Can you fill in this grid in less than 60 seconds?

×	4	9	1	7	3	5	2	8	6	10
1										

Number of seconds ....

4 Can you fill in this grid in less than 50 seconds?

×	5	10	3	8	1	4	9	6	2	7
1										

Number of seconds ....

My Time Graph

Grid 2										
Grid 3										
Grid 4										
	10 or less	20	30	40	50	60	70	80	90	100 or more

Number of seconds

Set 6: Check-up

Before we move on to explore groups of 0, let's check how much you remember about multiplying by groups of 1, 2, 5, 10 and doubling.

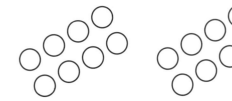

1 How many objects?

a 3 groups of 5 = ...

b .... groups of .... = ...

c .... groups of .... = ...

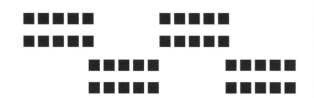

d .... groups of .... = ...

2 Circle the number which is the answer to the number sentence.

    a 9 × 1 =   10   9   7   **b** 5 × 10 =   50 55 15

    c 2 × 5 =   7 10   3   **d** 2 × 4 =   6   8 10

    e 9 × 2 =   18 19 11   **f** 4 × 10 = 14 50 40

3 Continue the counting patterns:

    a 37 36 35 ....

    b 30 28 26 ....

    c 120 110 100 ....

    d 85 80 75 ....

4 Do these quickly:

    a 1 × 10 = ...   **b** .... × 1 = 7   **c** 2 × .... = 18   **d** 1 × 5 = ...

    e 2 × .... = 12 **f** 4 × 5 = ...   **g** .... × 10 = 80 **h** 5 × .... = 10

Set 1: Groups of 0

Imagine you are at a zoo. You look carefully, but the elephant is not in its yard.

1 group of 0 elephants   or   1 × 0 = 0

You look carefully again.
The two tiger cages are empty.

2 groups of 0 tigers   or   2 × 0 = 0

1 Write the number sentence to match:

  a 3 palm trees with 0 monkeys   **b** 4 kennels with 0 dingoes

  .... × .... = ... × .... = ...

2 What do you notice? ....

3 Write the counting pattern for 0:

  0   0   0   ....

1	2	3	4	5	6	7	8	9	10
11	12	13	14	15	16	17	18	19	20
21	22	23	24	25	26	27	28	29	30
31	32	33	34	35	36	37	38	39	40
41	42	43	44	45	46	47	48	49	50
51	52	53	54	55	56	57	58	59	60
61	62	63	64	65	66	67	68	69	70
71	72	73	74	75	76	77	78	79	80
81	82	83	84	85	86	87	88	89	90
91	92	93	94	95	96	97	98	99	100

4 Notice that there is no pattern to colour on this number chart as all your numbers are 0.

You look very carefully. There are 10 glass cages but no snakes. Write the number sentence to match.

....

Set 2: Draw Groups of 0

Drawing groups of 'none' is easy.

For example, 5 groups of 0 sticks

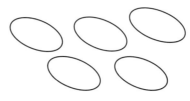

$5 \times 0 = 0$ sticks

1 Draw your own pictures to match. Write the number sentences too.

a 4 bowls with no flowers inside	**b** 2 streets with no cars on them

2 Find the match.
Draw lines to the correct answer.

2

3×0

4×0 5   0

3   5×0

2×0

3 Finish these number wheels.

a

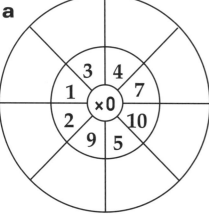

b

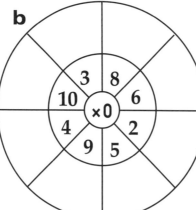

c

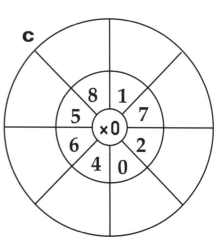

I am 6 × 0 added to 3 × 0. What number am I? ....

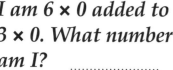

4 Challenge

a $5 \times \text{........} = 0$ **b** $9 \times 0 = \text{........}$ **c** $1 \times 0 = \text{........}$

d $10 \times \text{........} = 0$ **e** $8 \times 0 = \text{........}$ **f** $2 \times \text{........} = 0$

Number of seconds ....

Set 3: Mind Munchers

1 Write the number sentence to match each story.

a 7 horses with no riders on each horse.
How many riders?

.... × .... = ...

b 5 plates with no peas on each plate.
How many peas?

.... × .... = ...

Beat the clock

2 Can you fill in this grid in less than 30 seconds?

×	3	7	2	9	4	10	1	5	6	8
0										

Number of seconds ....

3 Can you fill in this grid in less than 30 seconds?

×	6	5	8	4	9	10	7	1	3	2
0										

Number of seconds ....

4 Make up three new grids of your own. Write your new times in seconds here:

a .... seconds   **b** .... seconds   **c** .... seconds

Circle your fastest time.

Set 4: Check-up

Before we move on to explore groups of 3, let's check how much you remember about multiplying groups of 0, 1, 2, 5 and 10.

1 Circle the number which is the answer to the number sentence.

a 8 × 1 =   10   9   8   **b** 2 × 6 =   8   10   12

c 10 × 2 =   20   12   8   **d** 8 × 5 =   20   40   13

e 7 × 10 =   17   70   77   **f** 10 × 0 =   10   9   0

2 Continue the counting patterns.

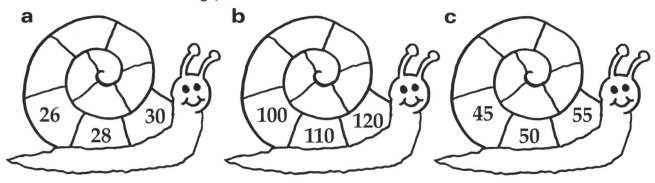

a 26   28   30

b 100   110   120

c 45   50   55

3 Do these quickly.

a 3 × .... = 30   **b** 4 × 1 = ...   **c** 9 × .... = 18   **d** 6 × 0 = ...

e 9 × 1 = ...   **f** .... × 5 = 25   **g** 7 × 10 = ...   **h** .... × 2 = 10

4 Finish these number wheels.

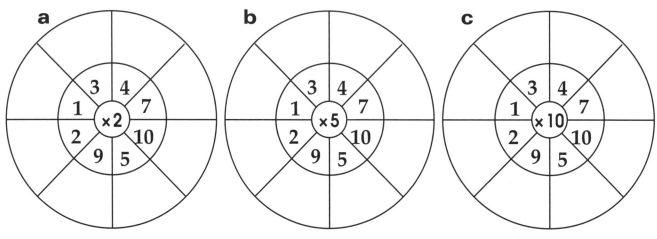

a ×2   3 4 1 7 2 10 9 5

b ×5   3 4 1 7 2 10 9 5

c ×10   3 4 1 7 2 10 9 5

Set 1: Groups of 3

What do you know that comes in 3s?
(For example, wheels on a tricycle, triplets ...) ....

1 There are 3 sides on a triangle.

3   1 group of .... sides = ... sides

2 How many sides on 2 triangles?

3 + 3   .... groups of .... sides = ... sides

3 How many sides on 3 triangles?

.... + ... + ... groups of .... sides = ... sides

4 How many sides on 4 triangles?

........+ .... + ... + ... groups of .... sides = ... sides

5 Write what you see here.

.... groups of .... = ...

6 Write how you count by 3.

3   6   ....

How many children altogether in 2 sets of triplets and 1 set of twins? ....

Set 2: Rows of 3

You can sort things into equal rows of 3 to make a 3s array. The things line up in rows and columns. This is what 10 rows of 3 butterflies look like as an array.

1 Draw 3 rows of 3 circles as an array.

2 Draw 5 rows of 3 triangles as an array.

3 Draw 7 rows of 3 rectangles as an array.

4 Draw 9 rows of 3 sticks as an array.

5 This is what 10 equal groups of 3 look like on a number line.

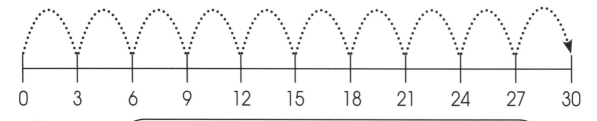

0 3 6 9 12 15 18 21 24 27 30

Draw your own jumps of 3 on this number line, starting at 0 and finishing at 30.

0 3 6 9 12 15 18 21 24 27 30

Set 3: *More About 3*

Write the number sentences to match.

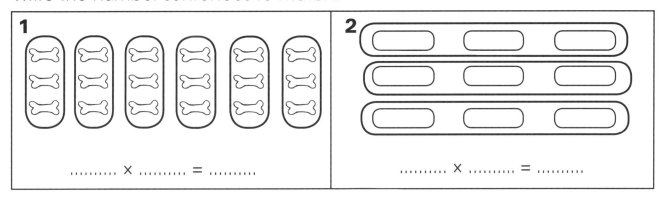

1

.... × .... = ...

2

.... × .... = ...

3 Colour in all the numbers as you count by 3.
What pattern can you see in the final digits?

1	2	3	4	5	6	7	8	9	10
11	12	13	14	15	16	17	18	19	20
21	22	23	24	25	26	27	28	29	30
31	32	33	34	35	36	37	38	39	40
41	42	43	44	45	46	47	48	49	50
51	52	53	54	55	56	57	58	59	60
61	62	63	64	65	66	67	68	69	70
71	72	73	74	75	76	77	78	79	80
81	82	83	84	85	86	87	88	89	90
91	92	93	94	95	96	97	98	99	100

Can you count by 3s with your eyes shut? ....
What's the biggest number you can count to by 3s? ....

4 Start at 18 and count back by 3s to 9. ....

5 Start at 30 and count back by 3s to 18. ....

6 Fill in the missing numbers.

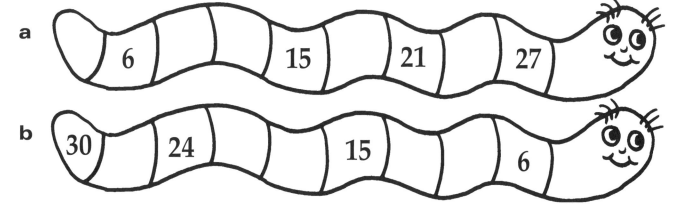

a 6 15 21 27

b 30 24 15 6

Set 4: What a Lot of Dragons!

How many?
Guess first. Circle groups of 3 and count.

1   My guess   ....

After counting   .... × 3 = ...

2   My guess   ....

After counting   .... × 3 = ...

3 Draw your own picture to match.
Write the number sentence.

> 5 bags with 3 marbles in each bag.
>
>
> .... × .... = ...

4 Join the dots in order.

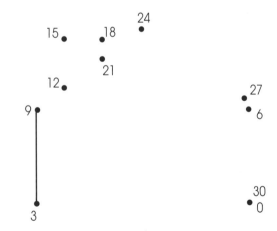

> *One mango costs $3.*
> *How much for 7 mangoes?*   ....

Set 5: Find the Match

1 Draw lines to the correct answer.

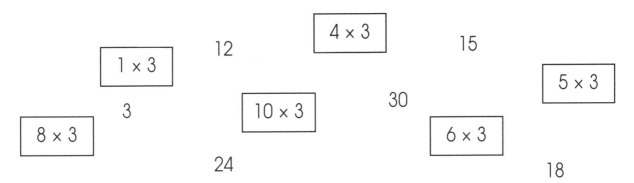

12   4 × 3   15

1 × 3

3   10 × 3   30   5 × 3

8 × 3   6 × 3

24   18

2 Find the answers then solve the riddle below using the code.

N: 8 × 3 = ...   O: 7 × 3 = ...   C: 9 × 3 = ...   S: 5 × 3 = ...

U: 6 × 3 = ...   A: 4 × 3 = ...   P: 2 × 3 = ...   T: 3 × 3 = ...

3 What cat has eight legs?

....
12   24   21   27   9   21   6   18   15   15

Challenge

4 Time yourself to see how quickly you can find the answers.

  a 9 × 3 = ...   **b** 6 × 3 = ...   **c** 3 × 3 = ...   **d** 7 × 3 = ...

  e 5 × 3 = ...   **f** 10 × 3 = ...   **g** 8 × 3 = ...   **h** 2 × 3 = ...

Number of seconds ....

5 Fill in this grid as quickly as you can.

×	4	7	3	1	2	5	8	6	9	10
3										

Number of seconds ....

Set 6: Beat the Clock

1 Can you fill in this grid in less than 80 seconds?

×	6	1	9	4	7	2	5	3	10	8
3										

Number of seconds ………

2 Can you fill in this grid in less than 70 seconds?

×	10	5	3	2	7	9	6	4	8	1
3										

Number of seconds ………

3 Can you fill in this grid in less than 60 seconds ?

×	2	7	1	9	5	8	6	10	4	3
3										

Number of seconds ………

4 Can you fill in this grid in less than 50 seconds ?

×	4	7	0	3	8	5	2	9	1	6
3										

Number of seconds ………

My Time Graph

	10 or less	20	30	40	50	60	70	80	90	100 or more
Grid 1										
Grid 2										
Grid 3										
Grid 4										

Number of seconds

Set 7: Mind Munchers

Write the number sentence to match each story.

---

1 4 cats with 3 whiskers each. How many whiskers?

.... × .... = ...

2 9 boats with 3 sails each. How many sails?

.... × .... = ...

3 6 logs with 3 mice in each one. How many mice?

.... × .... = ...

4 I save $3 each week. How much do I save in 7 weeks?

.... × .... = ...

Challenge

---

5 Each squirrel has 3 nuts. There are 30 nuts altogether. How many squirrels?

.... × .... = ...

6 Each flower has 3 petals. I counted 15 petals altogether. How many flowers do I have?

.... × .... = ...

---

7 Make up your own number story and write it here: ....

....

Write the number sentence for your story.

.... × .... = ...

Set 8: Check-up

Before we move on to explore groups of 4, let's check how much you remember about multiplying with 0, 1, 2, 3, 5 and 10.

Draw a picture to match.

1 6 × 3 = ...	**2** 5 × 0 = ...

3 Match the number names.

7 × 10   21   7 × 3   5 × 5   14   9 × 0

15   3 × 5   70   0   2 × 7   25

4 Finish these number wheels.

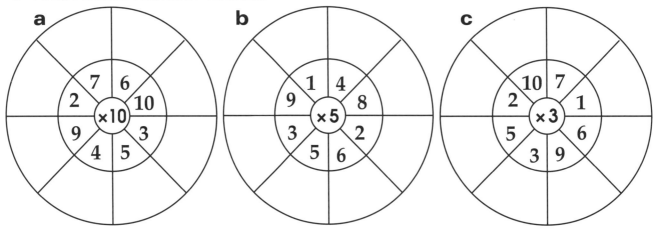

a ×10: 7 6 2 10 9 3 4 5

b ×5: 1 4 9 8 3 2 5 6

c ×3: 10 7 2 1 5 6 3 9

5 Do these quickly.

a .... × 1 = 8   **b** 8 × .... = 24   **c** 3 × .... = 15   **d** 9 × .... = 0

e 7 × .... = 21   **f** .... × 2 = 20   **g** 7 × .... = 7   **h** 3 × .... = 6

Four cakes cost $12.
How much for 1 cake? ....

Set 1: Groups of 4

1 What can you count that comes in fours?
(For example: legs on a cat, sides on a square) ....

There are 4 legs on 1 cow.
4

1 group of 4 legs = $\boxed{4}$ legs

2 How many legs on 2 dogs?
4 + 4

2 groups of 4 legs = ☐ legs

3 How many legs on 3 zebras?
4 + 4 + 4

3 groups of 4 legs = ☐ legs

4 How many sides on 4 squares?
4 + 4 + 4 + 4 ☐ ☐ ☐ ☐

4 groups of 4 sides = ☐ sides

5 How many wheels on 5 cars?
4 + 4 + 4 + 4 +4

5 groups of 4 wheels = ☐ wheels

6 Write what you see here.

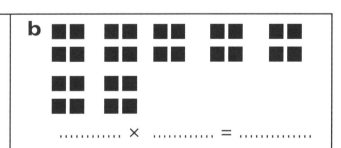

a .... × .... = ...

b .... × .... = ...

7 Finish this counting by 4s number pattern.

4   8   12   ....

I am sitting on a chair at a table. My dog is beside me. How many legs are there altogether? ....

Set 2: Rows of 4

You can sort things into equal rows of 4 to make a 4s array. The things line up in rows and columns. This is what 10 rows of 4 cats look like as an array.

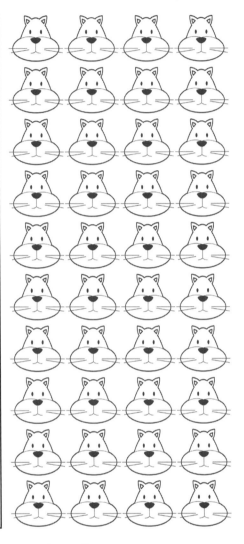

| **1** Draw 2 rows of 4 squares in an array. | **2** Draw 4 rows of 4 pentagons in an array. |
| **3** Draw 6 rows of 4 hexagons in an array. | **4** Draw 8 rows of 4 dots in an array. |

5 This is what 10 equal groups of 4 look like on a number line.

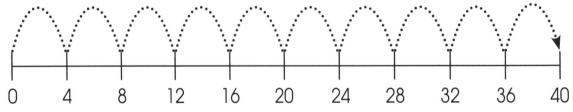

0   4   8   12   16   20   24   28   32   36   40

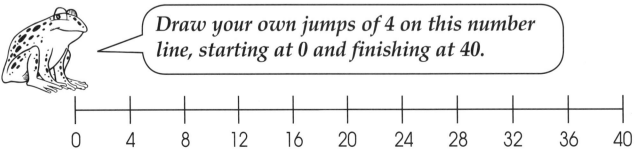

Draw your own jumps of 4 on this number line, starting at 0 and finishing at 40.

0   4   8   12   16   20   24   28   32   36   40

Set 3: Look for a Pattern

1 Colour in all the numbers as you count by 4. How many patterns can you see? What is the pattern of the final digits? ....

1	2	3	4	5	6	7	8	9	10
11	12	13	14	15	16	17	18	19	20
21	22	23	24	25	26	27	28	29	30
31	32	33	34	35	36	37	38	39	40
41	42	43	44	45	46	47	48	49	50
51	52	53	54	55	56	57	58	59	60
61	62	63	64	65	66	67	68	69	70
71	72	73	74	75	76	77	78	79	80
81	82	83	84	85	86	87	88	89	90
91	92	93	94	95	96	97	98	99	100

2 What's the second number in this pattern?

....

3 What's the eighth number in this pattern?

....

4 What's the tenth number in this pattern?

....

Challenge

5 Time yourself to see how quickly you can find the answers.

a 4 × 4 = ... **b** 7 × 4 = ... **c** 1 × 4 = ... **d** 2 × 4 = ...

e 8 × 4 = ... **f** 10 × 4 = ... **g** 5 × 4 = ... **h** 9 × 4 = ...

Number of seconds ....

6 Complete these number wheels:

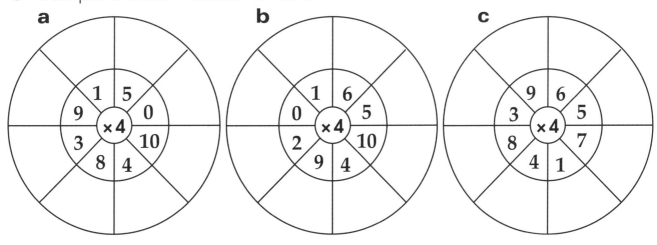

a ×4: 1, 5, 0, 10, 4, 8, 3, 9

b ×4: 1, 6, 5, 10, 4, 9, 2, 0

c ×4: 9, 6, 5, 7, 1, 4, 8, 3

Set 4: Beat the Clock

1 Can you fill in this grid in less than 80 seconds?

×	5	2	10	1	4	6	8	7	0	9
4										

Number of seconds ....

2 Can you fill in this grid in less than 70 seconds?

×	10	3	7	4	0	5	2	9	1	6
4										

Number of seconds ....

3 Can you fill in this grid in less than 60 seconds?

×	2	9	0	6	3	8	10	7	4	1
4										

Number of seconds ....

4 Can you fill in this grid in less than 50 seconds?

×	9	0	8	1	10	2	4	5	3	7
4										

Number of seconds ....

My Time Graph

Grid 1										
Grid 2										
Grid 3										
Grid 4										
	10 or less	20	30	40	50	60	70	80	90	100 or more

Number of seconds

Set 5: *Mind Munchers*

Write the number sentence to match each story.

1 3 dogs with 4 bones each.
How many bones altogether?

……… × ……… = ………

2 10 snacks at $4 each.
How much altogether?

……… × ……… = ………

3 7 birds with 4 worms each.
How many worms altogether?

……… × ……… = ………

4 5 tables with 4 legs each.
How many legs altogether?

……… × ……… = ………

Challenge

5 There are 36 sides altogether.
How many squares are there?

……… × ……… = ………

6 I counted 20 wheels altogether.
How many cars?

……… × ……… = ………

7 Make up your own number story and write it here:

....

....

Write the number sentence for your story.   ……… × ……… = ………

*Our naughty dog bites every 4th postman.
So far he has bitten 3.
How many postmen have visited us?*

Set 6: Check-up

Let's check how much you remember about multiplying by 0, 1, 2, 3, 4, 5 and 10.

1 Complete these number wheels.

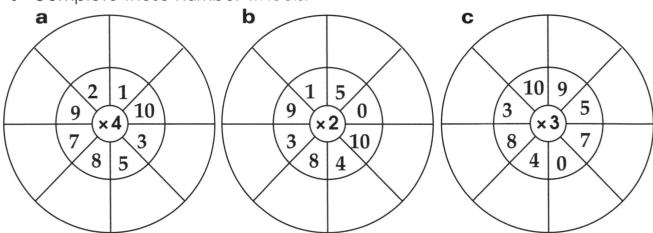

a

×4 with 2, 1, 10, 3, 5, 8, 7, 9

b

×2 with 1, 5, 0, 10, 4, 8, 3, 9

c

×3 with 10, 9, 5, 7, 0, 4, 8, 3

2 Do these in less than one minute.

a 2 × 9 = ...   **b** .... × 3 = 18   **c** 2 × .... = 0   **d** 9 × 4 = ...

e .... × 5 =10   **f** .... × 1 = 9   **g** 7 × .... = 14   **h** 7 × 10 = ...

3 Fill in each grid in less than 50 seconds.

a

×	9	8	1	10	2	4	5	3	7	6
4										

b

×	7	5	0	10	8	4	2	3	1	9
3										

c

×	3	8	1	10	2	4	5	9	7	6
5										

d

×	8	1	10	3	0	2	9	4	7	6
10										

Set 1: Extra Ideas

Games with Playing Cards

You will need:

- 8 small cards labelled × 0, × 1, × 2, × 3, × 4, × 5, × 10 and 'double' (photocopy page 72).
- A pack of playing cards with the picture cards removed.
- A timer.

◆ Wild Groups

Shuffle the large and small cards separately and place them face down. Turn over a playing card (for example, 6). Turn over a small card (for example, × 5). Multiply the two numbers together (for example, 6 × 5). Record question and answer in the spaces. Place the used cards at the bottom of each pile and start again. Repeat until you have had 8 turns.

1 ...... × ...... = ...   **2** ...... × ...... = ...   **3** ...... × ...... = ...   **4** ...... × ...... = ...

5 ...... × ...... = ...   **6** ...... × ...... = ...   **7** ...... × ...... = ...   **8** ...... × ...... = ...

◆ Race the Clock

Shuffle the playing cards and place them face down. Shuffle the small cards too.
Turn over a small card (for example, double). This is the multiplier for this round. Time yourself. Turn over the playing cards one by one and say the answer aloud (for example, double 8 is 16).
How long does it take to answer all 40 cards?

Drill Wheels

Photocopy the master on page 73 to create your own daily practice wheels. Fill in the number operation in the centre (for example, × 5) and write 8 random numbers from 0–10 around the middle section of each wheel. Now test yourself every day until you feel confident you know your multiplication tables.

Beat the Clock Grids

Photocopy the master on page 73 to create your own daily practice grids. In the lower left box write a number: 0, 1, 2, 3, 4, 5 or 10. On the top row, record random numbers from 0 to 10. Your answers go in the bottom row.

Multiplication Reference Tables

Photocopy the masters on pages 74 and 75. Use these for quick reference. Cover up one of the columns and time yourself saying the missing numbers.

Set 2: Extra Ideas

Teach your Calculator to Count

Remember that all multiplication is just repeated addition of the same number.

If you press the following buttons on your calculator, you can practise counting by each multiple for as long as you like.

To count forwards by 2s press (2) (+) (2) (=)

Just keep pressing the (+) (2) (=) buttons. Try to say the next multiple before you press (=).

To count backwards by 2s press (2) (0) (−) (2) (=)

To count forwards by 10s press (1) (0) (+) (1) (0) (=)

To count backwards by 10s press (1) (0) (0) (−) (1) (0) (=)

To count forwards by 5s press (5) (+) (5) (=)

To count backwards by 5s press (5) (0) (−) (5) (=)

To count forwards by 3s press (3) (+) (3) (=)

To count backwards by 3s press (3) (0) (−) (3) (=)

To count forwards by 4s press (4) (+) (4) (=)

To count backwards by 4s press (4) (0) (−) (4) (=)

Counting multiples like this will help you remember your tables facts too.

Set 3: Extra Ideas

Parents: Ideas for Using the Internet

Tables websites

There are many free websites to help your child practise their tables online. Some examples you can try are:

◆ www.thatquiz.org

◆ www.mathisfun.com/quiz

The best sites will tell you how many tables facts your child successfully answered and also the time it took them to complete the quiz. You are aiming for flexibility, speed and accuracy.

Smartphone and ipad apps

Look online for an app you like the look of. Again the best apps will tell you how many tables facts your child successfully answered and also their time. You are aiming for flexibility, speed and accuracy.

Mindmaps

Encourage your child to create their own concept map online, showing everything they know about their multiplication tables. For example, try using:

◆ https://bubbl.us

Vodcasts

Your child might like to design a rap song to help them remember their tables, say for × 4. Film them and vodcast it (e.g. using Quicktime Pro), or tape them and podcast it (e.g. using Audacity).

Playing Cards

x 0

x 1

x 2

x 3

x 4

x 5

x 10

double

Excel Basic Skills *Times Tables 1 Years 2–3* Unit 9

Drill Wheels

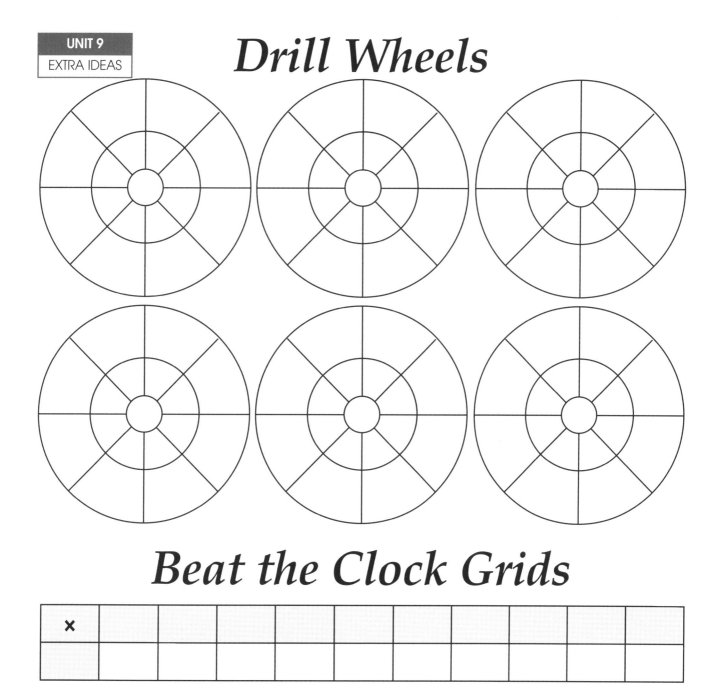

Beat the Clock Grids

×									

Number of seconds ....

×									

Number of seconds ....

×									

Number of seconds ....

Reference Tables

Groups of 0

0 × 0	0
1 × 0	0
2 × 0	0
3 × 0	0
4 × 0	0
5 × 0	0
6 × 0	0
7 × 0	0
8 × 0	0
9 × 0	0
10 × 0	0

Groups of 1

0 × 1	0
1 × 1	1
2 × 1	2
3 × 1	3
4 × 1	4
5 × 1	5
6 × 1	6
7 × 1	7
8 × 1	8
9 × 1	9
10 × 1	10

Groups of 2

0 × 2	0
1 × 2	2
2 × 2	4
3 × 2	6
4 × 2	8
5 × 2	10
6 × 2	12
7 × 2	14
8 × 2	16
9 × 2	18
10 × 2	20

Groups of 3

0 × 3	0
1 × 3	3
2 × 3	6
3 × 3	9
4 × 3	12
5 × 3	15
6 × 3	18
7 × 3	21
8 × 3	24
9 × 3	27
10 × 3	30

Reference Tables

Groups of 4

0 × 4	0
1 × 4	4
2 × 4	8
3 × 4	12
4 × 4	16
5 × 4	20
6 × 4	24
7 × 4	28
8 × 4	32
9 × 4	36
10 × 4	40

Groups of 5

0 × 5	0
1 × 5	5
2 × 5	10
3 × 5	15
4 × 5	20
5 × 5	25
6 × 5	30
7 × 5	35
8 × 5	40
9 × 5	45
10 × 5	50

Groups of 10

0 × 10	0
1 × 10	10
2 × 10	20
3 × 10	30
4 × 10	40
5 × 10	50
6 × 10	60
7 × 10	70
8 × 10	80
9 × 10	90
10 × 10	100

Doubles

2 × 0	0
2 × 1	2
2 × 2	4
2 × 3	6
2 × 4	8
2 × 5	10
2 × 6	12
2 × 7	14
2 × 8	16
2 × 9	18
2 × 10	20

My Progress Chart

Excel Basic Skills *Times Tables 1 Years 2–3* Unit 9